PLANTS WE EAT AND WEAR

An illustrated key to the plants upon which man is directly dependent for his food and clothing, with some essential facts about each plant.

by

H. E. JAQUES
Sometime Professor of Biology
Iowa Wesleyan College

DOVER PUBLICATIONS, INC., NEW YORK

Published in Canada by General Publishing Company, Ltd., 30 Lesmill Road, Don Mills, Toronto, Ontario.

Published in the United Kingdom by Constable and Company, Ltd., 10 Orange Street, London WC 2.

This Dover edition, first published in 1975, is an unabridged and slightly corrected republication of the work originally published by the author, at Mount Pleasant, Iowa, in 1943.

International Standard Book Number: 0-486-22563-1
Library of Congress Catalog Card Number: 74-12656

Manufactured in the United States of America
Dover Publications, Inc.
180 Varick Street
New York, N. Y. 10014

INTRODUCTION

"here and when do we eat; what shall we wear?" Much of our wakeful hours are filled with attention to these matters.

All life on our planet is directly or indirectly dependent upon the green plants for food. That requires the some 160,000 different green plants to not only provide their own organic foods but in like manner to make and supply nearly 100,000 non-green plants and about 900,000 kinds of animals with organic foods. It is a large task, but in one way or another every one of the 160,000 is doing its part.

It seems strange that man in his long experience with plants has learned to use so few of them for his most essential needs. In the following pages, plants contributing to our every-day menu are pictured and described. The list has been checked and re-checked to include all important ones.

More than 500 families of plants are listed in "Plant Families, - How to Know Them" but the plants treated in this book fall in only seventy of these families. It would seem safe to say that fully 95% of man's plant foods come from representatives of only five families.

Leaf the list through and count the plants you have eaten within the past month. Our modesty in calling upon the great wealth of the world's plants is amazing.

The case of plants used to "wear" is even more strange. Not counting the Elm barrel which the poker player is purported to sometimes wear home, we could find only twenty-seven plants related in any important way to our clothing needs.

Of course we have not attempted to account for all the strange plants eaten by savage tribes, the wild fruits and fibers used of necessity by pioneers, or the plants tried occasionally by nature lovers. The list is fairly complete, though of course, some of you will feel that another plant or two should have been included. We hope it gives the food lover a better knowledge of plants and the plant student a fuller conception of what he eats.

We've had the help of many friends again. Francesca Jaques and Mary Hinkle have made most of the drawings. We are grateful to all these as well as to the many nature lovers and teachers who write to say nice things about the Pictured-Key Nature books.

January 15, 1943

CONTENTS

NOW, PLANTS ARE LIKE THIS!

Some knowledge of plant structures and plant classification is necessary to make any intelligent study of plants. Without teaching a whole course in Botany, we will attempt to explain some things the young plant lover should find helpful as he pursues the rest of the book.

The world's grand array of more than 250,000 different plants divides rather naturally into four great divisions. More than half of these plants bear flowers and seeds; the others do not. These others usually have single celled "spores" for their reproduction. Let's mark off a section then, and label it "Spermatophyta (The Seed-bearing Plants) 130,000+."

If a city is to attain size it must have adequate water, sewerage and transportation systems that extend to all parts of it. That is equally true for plants. In them these three systems are combined and known as fibro-vascular-bundles. The seed-bearing plants, of course, are thus equipped, but another group, the ferns, also have vascular bundles. That gives us our second division which we will label "Pteridophyta (Ferns) 4,500+." All these interesting plants have vascular bundles but do not have seeds.

Now, the going gets more technical. The seed plants and ferns, and also some others, reproduce by an egg which is in a cellular flask-shaped structure that botanists call an archegonium. Many very simple plants on the other hand produce eggs that are surrounded only by a non-cellular cell wall and have never known an archegonium. This gives us a natural separation for the remaining

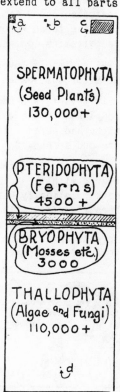

Figure 1. The whole Plant Kingdom (250,000 different plants) divided proportionately into its four great divisions. a, representing the 279 seed-bearing plants used for food, described in this book; b, seed-bearing plants used for clothing, (27); c, Sturtevant's maximum number of food plants, all divisions, (4233); d, algae and fungi used for food, (12).

5

plants. Those with archegonia (but no vascular bundles) we will label "Bryophyta (Mosses and Liverworts) 3,000." All the remaining plants, - the "have-nots" - which have no archegonia, no vascular bundles and no seeds, we'll call "Thallophyta (Algae and Fungi) 110,000+." As plants live and do their work, this last one is an exceedingly important group but man uses only a very few of the plants within it for his food.

We make practically no use at all of the Ferns or of the Mosses for clothing or food. But the Seed-bearing Plants - that is different - how very much we depend upon them!

HOW WE FEEL ABOUT FOOD

The trend of thought about our food has undergone some radical changes in recent years. Not so long ago the chief emphasis with foods was taste and perhaps next its appearance. Now we hear much about better health, physical appearance, and vitality. Foods are selected and recommended for the nutriment man's digestive system can take from them. The discussion runs to calories and vitamins with the result that many of us are eating the foods we once disliked, because they provide the desired vitamins or enable us to maintain the proper weight.

Bailey in his inventories lists 247 vegetables and 161 fruits a total of 408, eaten some where the world around.

Sturtevant, who some years ago made a list of the cultivated food plants of the world, named 1070 species but went on to say that he had noted a total of 4233 plants which were used some - where and somehow for food.

These larger lists which are still surprisingly small as compared with the total species of known plants, include many plants practically unknown in our country and numbers of others ("weeds" to the layman) which are non-poisonous and nutritive of course, but only occasionally included in a mess of greens or tried for jellies, preserves, etc., for the novelty of the thing. Recently the writer was served Milkweed

stems, the tender young shoots having been prepared like creamed asparagus. (In this case the plant supplied the milk and the cook the cream.) We enjoyed it, for we like to try out new plant possibilities, but we did not come home and dig up our asparagus bed and plant our Milkweeds instead.

The whole food problem boils down to this, - **The green plants first make their own food and grow, so that they can feed the entire living world.** Let us see just how they "make their own food" and what they do with it.

HOW PLANTS FEED AND GROW

A growing green plant is truthfully said to be the "greatest factory in the world." It is a factory where chemical activities are busily transforming available compounds or elements into new compounds in some marvelous ways and with a mass production that puts our assembly lines to shame.

The raw materials needed are few and almost everywhere abundant. Practically all of the many products the plant makes are made from ten elements, Carbon, Oxygen, Hydrogen, Nitrogen, Phosporous, Sulphur, Iron, Magnesium, Calcium and Potassium. Other elements may play their part in very small portions in some plant products, but the 10 just named are the elements that figure most largely in plant growth.

The plant begins its work with the first three elements named above. Hydrogen and oxygen are taken in through the roots in the form of water, (H_2O). Carbon and oxygen are taken into the leaves from the surrounding air as a gas, carbon dioxide (CO_2). The power is sun-light. It is wireless. It streams into the factory with high efficiency and is not even metered. Innumerable tiny green bodies within the cells of the leaf make up the

the personnel. With a bit of plant magic which botanists call photosynthesis, these very simple, thin and highly abundant substances, - water and carbon dioxide, are fused into a new product, glucose, one of the sugars. Chemically it is expressed thus:

$$6\ CO_2 + 6\ H_2O \rightarrow C_6H_{12}O_6 + 6\ O_2$$

(six molecules of carbon dioxide + six molecules of water

Figure 2. Photosynthesis of plants, and respiration of plants and animals balance the air and water for healthful living.

yield by this change one molecule of glucose plus six molecules
of oxygen). This extra oxygen is interesting and very important.
It is put back into the air and is used again by animals and
plants in respiration. Thus the green plants of country and
town, - park or window box - are releasing oxygen into the surrounding air throughout the lighted hours and so making the air
more healthful. That is why we put some green plants in our
fish bowl. The plant gives off oxygen in its photosynthesis
which is dissolved into the water. The fish utilizing this
oxygen for its respiration, returns carbon dioxide to the water
which, of course, is used by the plants again for photosynthesis

The energy of the sun is required to compound the glucose.
This energy is released again when the glucose or some later
plant product made from it, is broken down by respiration. And
thus the fish gets its power to move and grow, and we maintain
our body temperature of $98.6°$ F., and get the necessary energy
to work and play and to think through (not too dull, we hope)
pages like these.

The plant, still utilizing the sun's energy, directly or
indirectly, can shift the proportions of the elements in the
glucose and change it into many similar compounds such as cane
sugar ($C_6H_{22}O_{11}$) or starch ($C_6H_{10}O_5$) or by more radical shifts,
into fats and oils, all of which also contain only these three
elements. A typical fat formula is that of palmitin ($C_{51}H_{98}O_6$).
Since it takes additional sun-energy to change carbo-hydrates
into fats, it is apparent that fats when broken down by respiration will release more energy than can be had from carbo-
hydrates.

MAKING PLANT PROTEINS

Proteins contain not only carbon, hydrogen, and oxygen, as
do carbo-hydrates and fats but also nitrogen and usually either
phosporus or sulphur or both. The plant of course makes its
own proteins by building over carbo-hydrates and adding the
necessary new elements. Protein compounds are very complex.
Typical formulas to illustrate this are gliadin, a wheat protein, ($C_{685}H_{1068}N_{196}O_{211}S_5$) and casein from milk,
($C_{708}H_{1130}N_{180}O_{224}S_4P_4$). The living protoplasm of plant and
animal cells is formed of proteins. Since it seems that
animal proteins can be made only from plant proteins these
plant compounds assume increased significance.

The other elements already referred to become parts of some
special plant products.

MOVEMENTS OF FOODS

Just as a commercial factory has its pipe lines, belt lines or other schemes of transportation to bring in raw materials and to move the finished product to storage, plants are likewise equipped. Since all plant products, raw or finished, are moved as liquids, pipe lines suffice. Water containing the needed plant foods dissolved in it, is taken into the tiny root tips by osmotic pressure and shortly finds its way into small tubes made from elongated cylindrical cells placed end to end. As the tiny roots unite into larger roots, the tubes collect into larger bundles so that when the several large roots fuse into the plant stem many fibrovascular bundles, each with several to numerous liquid-carrying tubes are running parallel through the length of the stem. These again separate as they pass into the branches of the plant. A few pass out each leaf, flower or fruit stem, and then splitting up more and more until all parts of the leaf, flower or fruit are served. The veins seen in leaves are these bundles. Some of the tubes carry raw materials into the leaves and other tubes in the same bundle will transport organized foods out.

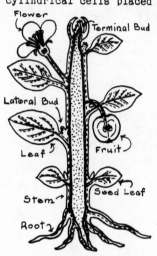

Figure 3. Diagram of plant to show parts and the vascular system. Solid lines to carry liquids up; dotted lines carrying them down.

Most of the photosynthesis of foods goes on in the leaves, although any green plant-part such as green stems, green fruit, or even green tubers will be doing their quota of this important work. During the day the leaves fill up with the foods being organized within them. Day and night the pipe lines are carrying this away to the ware-houses for storage or to parts of the plant where these organized foods are being built into new plant parts. Simple sugar or starch tests can be made which reveal that leaves contain much more starch and sugar towards the end of a day than at its beginning.

FOOD STORAGE

Plants usually store food to provide for a time when the plant will need it. Fleshy tap roots such as Beets, fleshy lateral roots as the Sweet potato, thick stems as in

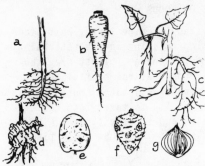

Figure 4. Special storage organs.
a, fibrous roots; b, fleshy taproot;
c, fleshy lateral root; d, rhizome (fleshy
stem); e, tuber (fleshy stem); f, corm
(fleshy stem); g, bulb (fleshy leaves).

Kohlrabi, tubers (special stems) as the Irish potato, rhizomes (root-like stems) as in Ginger, thick leaf-stems as Rhubarb and seeds are examples. These serve the plant for reproduction, or for quick growth in emergencies. All seeds contain sufficient food materials to supply the young plant till it can get on its own. Man has learned to take these for his own use. He is a robber when he does so because the plants meant them for themselves. If he is smart, he will not take all of them, or at least will make some adequate provision for assuring a big crop again and again. Only "dummies" kill the goose that lays the golden eggs, or digs orchids or any other scarce plants.

AT THE PAY WINDOW

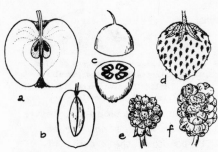

Figure 5. Some types of Fleshy Fruits.
a, pome; b, drupe; c, berry; d, fleshy
receptacle; e, aggregate fruit, f, multiple
fruit.

Plants have some jobs let out to others and are often willing to pay well for the work. Birds and other animals are engaged to scatter plant seeds. Such seeds are often enclosed in tasteful nutritious fruit in which much food material is stored. Blackberries and wild grapes, for instance, are widely scattered by birds dropping the undigested seeds. Larger fruits are carried away to be eaten in a secluded spot and the seeds rejected. Man makes good food uses of these fruits.

Fleshy leaves and stems are designed as storage organs but even slender parts may contain much food acceptable to man, as well as the vitamins we watch for. Just as we wish to give the best we possess to our children, so plants turn their most concentrated foods into their flowers and seeds. A seed is a young plant (embryo) which has enough concentrated food stored with it to provide nutriment for the little plant until it can establish a root system, become green and make an adequate amount of food to supply its own needs. Part of this rich supply of food is in the cotyledons or seed leaves. These cotyledons are a

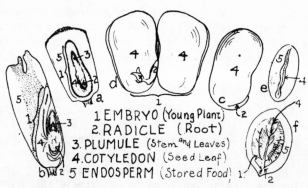

1 EMBRYO (Young Plant)
2. RADICLE (Root)
3. PLUMULE (Stem and Leaves)
4. COTYLEDON (Seed Leaf)
5 ENDOSPERM (Stored Food)

Figure 6. Typical seeds, and their parts. a, kernel of corn; b, transverse section of kernel of corn; c, Lima bean with seed coat removed; d, bean with cotyledons spread apart. Castor bean with seed coat removed; e, edge view; f, face view with half of endosperm removed.

part of the embryo. Often an endosperm surrounds the embryo. It is simply a mass of stored food which the young plant after it has started to grow digests and uses to build its own tissues. In seeds like the bean the endosperm has been consumed and made a part of the cotyledons before the seed ripens. There is no endosperm but instead two large cotyledons in beans. These supply food to the young plant. Corn, a monocotyledon has of course only one cotyledon. A very large percentage of the plant foods utilized by man, around the world, comes from seeds.

PLANT POISONS

While the eating of plants is being discussed something should be said of plant poisons. Just as man puts barbed wire or electric fences around his belongings, plants have found it necessary to erect barriers with the result that some plants are thorn covered and in consequence are untouched by grazing animals. Other plants have been protected by poisons; on the whole, however, this is a friendly world and the percentage of poisonous plants is small.

WEARING PLANTS

Out of necessity man was likely a big eater long before he gave much thought to things to wear, and even when he put on clothes for protection or ornament it was easier to kill then to weave. His first clothing was likely the skins of other animals.

11

The plants we wear make their contribution in several ways. Fibers are twisted into thread and woven into fabrics. Some of these fibers surround seeds to enable them to be wind disseminated. Man removes these threads and uses them for twisting without needing to give them much special treatment. Cotton is the outstanding example.

The stems of many species of plants contain long, very slim heavy walled fibers to give strength to the stem. These bast fibers are removed from the stem by "retting," (putting in water or laid out to take the dew) or a mechanical process, smoothed up, bleached, twisted into threads and woven. Linen from flax and ramie from an Indian plant illustrate this type. Fibers are also taken from the leaves of some plants.

Thick milky juice (latex) as found in some plants is collected and processed to form a tough water-proof material. Rubber from several plant sources illustrates this method. It and similar preparations are usually spread on a base of cotton or other fiber materials to give strength to the product.

Rayon threads are made from plant parts that are extensively processed, but that is likely carrying our matter too far, for only a step more and we would be considering the plants that feed the silkworms that in turn produce the silk fibers.

FLOWER PATTERNS

For the reader whose botanical training is limited, perhaps we should say a bit about flowers since flower structures are used so largely in determining plants. Complete flowers have four parts (all of which are modified leaves) arising in whorls from the end of a stem, the pedicel.

The expanded end of this stem is known as the receptacle. Going up the stem, the first whorl of parts is the calyx made of sepals. Occasionally flowers have a series of leaf-like bracts below the calyx. These sepals enclose the bud and protect its more delicate parts and are usually green in color, though not necessarily so. The next whorl

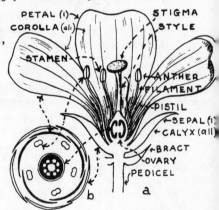

Figure 7. a, longitudinal section of a flower naming its parts; b, floral diagram of the same flower.

is the corolla, and its parts the petals. Petals are often brilliantly colored and fancifully marked. They attract insects and other pollinators. The petals of a corolla may be united with each other to form a tube; the same is true of sepals.

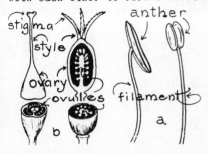

Stamens come next. They are the male reproductive parts and produce pollen in their anthers. Filaments are usually present to hold the anthers out from the walls of the flower. At the center of the flower perched on the end of the pedicel is the pistil. It is made up of ovary, style and stigma. It is the female part of the flower. In each of one

Figure 8. a, stamens showing parts; b, pistils dissected to show parts.

or more cavities of the ovary are borne one or more ovules. The stigma at the topmost part of the pistil is a special organ for receiving the pollen grains. It is usually separated from the ovary by a longer or short stem known as the style. Through the action of wind, insects or some other agency, pollen is transferred from anthers to stigmas. This process is polli- nation. The pollen grain then grows a tube which penetrating the stigma style and ovary, searches out an ovule and breaking into it releases a sperm nucleus which fuses with the egg nucleus of the ovule. This process is known as fertilization.

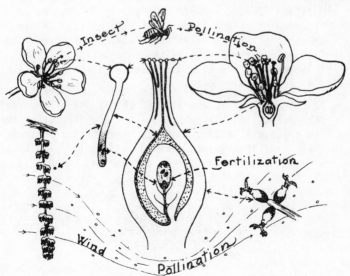

Figure 9. Pollination and fertilization work like this.

13

When it transpires successfully the ovule develops into a seed
and the ovary containing the ovule becomes a fruit. Only one
or two or three of these parts are present in some ("incom-
plete") flowers. Flowers with both stamens and pistils are
said to be perfect while if but one or the other of these "essential organs" are represented in the flower it is imperfect.
The whole story would cover several additional pages but this
should enable the novice to get started. The study of plants
is interesting and we recommend it just for the fun it offers.
Some other terms relating to plant structures are defined in
the glossary.

ABOUT PLANT NAMES

Every one of the more than 250,000 plants known to live on
the earth has a scientific name, which should be the same in
all languages and in all parts of the world. Many of the better known plants also have common names, - often several of
them for one plant, which makes the understanding difficult.

Throughout the book and in the "List" (p. 150) it will be
noted that emphasis has been given to the common name of each
plant but that its scientific name has been added, for in many
cases that is the only way one can be sure just which plant is
being discussed.

Scientific names always begin with a capitalized word. It
is the genus name. Closely similar plants fall in the same
genus and related genera belong to a "family." The second
word is the species name. We begin it with a small letter. A
third, - a variety name is sometimes included. A scientific
name is followed by the name (or its abbreviation) of the
scientist who gave this name to the plant. It is called the
"authority" or "author."

Take "Dent Corn" for an example; it is but one of six varieties of Zea (genus) mays (species). Its full scientific name
is Zea mays indentata Bailey. That tells us Bailey devised
this name and that the variety name is "indentata." Scientific
names are printed in italic type or underscored.

HOW TO USE THE KEYS

here is always a temptation to find plants in a book like this, by leafing through and looking at the pictures. That's often not so bad for much can be learned in that way. The experienced botanist or zoologist sometimes saves a lot of time in his identification work by turning to a group to which he knows his plant must belong, then by comparing pictures, selects a few species which represent all the ones which his unknown specimen could possibly be. From there it is a simple matter to carefully compare the key characters with his specimen and the determination is made.

Well planned identification keys makes the naming of plants or animals comparatively simple and accurate. Young nature lovers should train themselves to handle keys with ease and precision.

We see in a greenhouse a strange, coarse vine bearing several large somewhat banana-shaped fruits, 10 or 12 inches long, which are said to be edible. How can our key help us?

Starting at the first of the key at page 16 we compare 1a with 1b and noting the flowers on our plant, assign it to 1a and see at the right of the page that we are referred to the 7th pair of statements. Examining the plant again we see that while the leaves are long and broad and punctured with slits and holes, all the veins run somewhat parallel to each other. We can check farther if we wish and find that the other characters likewise agree, so we realize our plant is a "Monocotyledon" and examine 8a and 8b to find the leaves not palm-like and so turn to number 11. The nature of the flowers and fruit of our plant puts it in 11b and now sends us to number 29 to find the first statement agreeing with our plant. Comparing 30a with 30b, it is at once apparent that the plant in question is a Ceriman. We next check it with the description and picture and see that we are doubtless right.

As you work with these keys you will find that many plants appear at two or more places in the key. Many species have been keyed both by their use and by their botanical characters to make the determination more sure. If you are not a botanist look up the unfamiliar terms in the illustrated glossary at the back and the rest should be easy.

PICTURED KEYS FOR IDENTIFYING
THE PLANTS WE EAT AND WEAR

1a   Plants at sometime in their life bearing flowers and seeds. **7**

1b   Plants not producing flowers or seeds. **2**

2a   Plants at least a few inches in height and formed of many cells. **3**

2b   Microscopic single celled plants used to raise bread; eaten for their vitamins. Fig. 10.

           YEAST   Saccharomyces cerevisiae Han

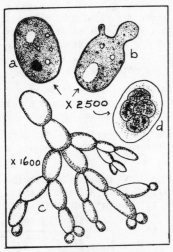

a, single plant; b, cell producing 2 buds; c, a colony of budded cells; d, a cell containing four resting spores (ascospores within an ascus).

There are a number of species of yeasts but this one which is used rather exclusively in bread-making and beer-brewing is the most important. Yeast plants grow and multiply by budding. Resting spores are also formed sometimes within a cell. This type of spore formation shows the yeasts to be Ascomycetes.

Yeasts are rich in vitamins.

Yeasts change sugar into carbon dioxide and alcohol. It is this gas that makes dough rise and gives the effervescence to fermented beverages. Wild yeasts are abundant and widely distributed. The wild yeasts found on the skins of fruit bring about prompt fermentation when the juice is extracted from such fruit. "Salt-rising" bread depends upon wild yeasts and bacteria for its leavening.

It is interesting to note that the large percentage of gluten in wheat is what makes wheat flour superior for bread making. The gluten holds the carbon dioxide gas until the bread raises and is baked. Kneading the bread dough breaks the large gas bubbles up into many tiny ones and makes the bread finer grained.

Flours that are short on gluten cannot hold the gas and do not raise well.

3a   Much branched marine plants, yellowish-brown, or reddish-purple. **4**

3b   Land plants, often without chlorophyll. **5**

4a Mostly a Pacific Ocean red alga, without an auxiliary
cell (separate vegetative cell which receives the zygote
nucleus in its migration from the carpogonium). Fig. 11.

AGAR-AGAR Gelidium cartilagineum Gaill.

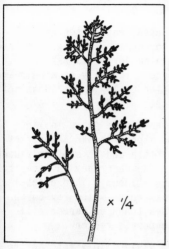

Figure 11

This is one of the several similar
species of red algae from which Agar-
agar is extracted. These plants grow
abundantly in the Pacific along both
the Asiatic and American coasts.
Agar is used in soups, jellies, ice
cream and medicines, usually to give
bulk. It is employed in the textile
industry and has proved an ideal
solidifier for culture media used in
the study of bacteria since its melt-
ing point is higher than that of
gelatine.

It has been produced largely by
the Japanese. In more recent years
it has been gathered and extracted in
our country. Some members of the
genus are found in the Atlantic.

This product is also known as vegetable-isinglass, Ceylon moss
or Chinese moss.

4b Red algae growing mostly along the shores of the North Sea
and the Atlantic coast. Usually shorter than 4a. An auxil-
lary cell present. Fig. 12.

IRISH MOSS (a) Chondrus crispus
Stac. (b) Gigartina mammillosa.

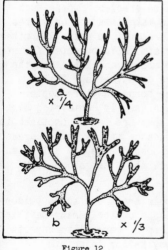

Figure 12

Both of these red algae have flattened, some-what ribbon-like thalli.
They are attached to the rocks by
branched root-like structures. After
being collected the plants are put
through several turns of washing and
drying. This Irish Moss or Carragheen, as it is sometimes called, is
made into a jelly or by using more
water, into a beverage.

The quantity of marine algae is
unlimited, but since its nutritive
value for man is comparatively low,
only a few species are much used
for food. These plants are now
collected in quantities off the New
England coast.

5a Whitish fleshy fruiting bodies growing on the ground or on decaying plants; never contain green chlorophyll; reproducing by spores. 6

5b Small grayish-green leaf-like plants growing on the ground. Spores born in shallow cups. Fig. 13.

ICELAND MOSS Cetraria islandica Ach.

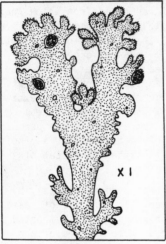

Figure 13

This lichen, rather common in Iceland and Norway, is dried, ground into flour and used for bread making. It is also made into jelly or a beverage. Its nutrition is low as man does not readily digest it.

The Manna-Lichen grows in large patches on stones in the deserts of Africa and Asia and is similarly used for food. Danish brandy is made from the Reindeer-Lichen. This species grows at its best in the far north but is often found on barren hilltops in temperate regions.

Lichens would likely rate as the world's sturdiest plants. They are really a dual partnership in which an algal plant has joined forces with a fungus.

6a A mushroom with sponge-like cap; spores born in cavities on outside of cap. Fig. 14.

COMMON MOREL Morchella esculenta Pers.

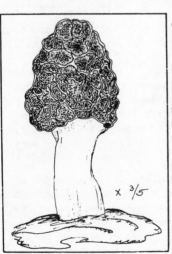

Figure 14

Some folks call this and the several related species "Sponge Mushrooms" and make them the only ones they will collect to eat. The other mushrooms are Basidiomycetes (bearing their spores on clubs) but the Morels are Ascomycetes. Their spores are borne in microscopic sacks, each usually containing eight spores. They are found sometimes in great abundance in low wooded areas. The honey-combed caps are yellowish-brown while the stems are nearly white.

No Morels are known to be poisonous. Because of their many cavities they need to be carefully inspected as they may harbor insects.

6b Mushrooms with umbrella-like head, pink gills, a collar around the stem and without a volva. Fig. 15.

COMMON MUSHROOM _Agaricus campestris_ L.

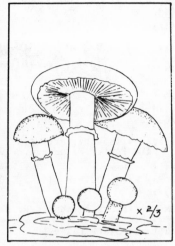

Figure 15

This is the usual species of mushroom sold on the market. It is frequently found in late summer and fall growing in fields. The gills are at first pink but turn brown when they age.

The vegetative part of these plants consists of many white threads (mycelia) growing through the ground where their nutriment is absorbed from decaying organic matter. Cultivated mushrooms are raised in caves or buildings where the temperature and humidity can be controlled. Pieces of spawn (mycelia) are planted in manure-enriched beds. When they first come up the head entirely surrounds the stem. They are then known as buttons.

There are hundreds of species of wild mushrooms which are edible and only a comparatively few which are poisonous. Since the poisonous ones are so deadly no one should ever gather and eat mushrooms unless he is sure of the species he has collected. There are much quicker methods of dying but few that are more painful.

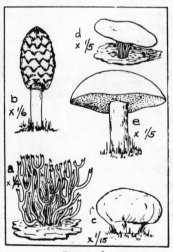

Figure 16

A few of the common edible wild species are being pictured. Unless you know your mushrooms DO NOT collect something that may somewhat resemble these drawings and feed them to your family. It's safer to take your chances with T.N.T.

Fig. 16. Some edible mushrooms.

a, CORAL FUNGUS, white, yellow or pink; b, SHAGGY MANE, several inches high, much prized; c, PUFFBALL, all puffballs are safe, but break them open to be sure they are puffballs; d, OYSTER MUSHROOM, white or cream, grows on trees; e, EDIBLE BOLETUS, red-brown on top, greenish beneath.

19

7a Leaves usually parallel-veined (a);
    flowering parts usually in 3's (b);
    stems with bundles scattered through-
    out or hollow; seeds with one cotyle-
    don. Fig. 17. The MONOCOTYLEDONS. .8

Figure 17

7b Leaves usually net veined (a); flow-
    ering parts usually in 5's (some-
    times 4's) (b); stems with bundles
    arranged in ring around the pith, or
    woody with outer bark; seeds with
    two cotyledons. Fig. 18. The
    DICOTYLEDONS. 42

Figure 18

THE MONOCOTYLEDONS

8a Plants with the palm-type of foliage, with very large pin-
    nate or palmate compound leaves. **PALM FAMILY** Palmaceae. . 9
8b Plants not having large palm-like leaves................ .11
9a Leaves pinnate or feather-like. See Figs. 20 and 21 . . .10
9b Leaves palmate or fan-like. Fig. 19.
                CHINESE FAN-PALM Livistona chinensis R. Br

a, young plant; b, flowers; c, fruit; d, Dwarf Palmetto.

Before a host of inventors, REA and other movements made it
possible for us to be fanned electrically one of the most ef-
ficient "coolers" was the palm-leaf fan, still used in many
regions. Palms fall into two classes; some have feather shaped
or pinnate leaves, while a smaller number have palmate leaves.
The center of a leaf of this latter kind was trimmed to convenient size and bound with two narrow strips of palm leaf to pre-
vent splitting down. The leaf petiole was cut to convenient
handle length. Drying, then, made the fan ready for the market.

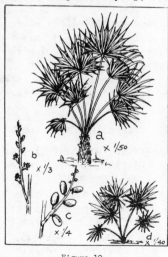

Figure 19

More attractive fans are made by
splitting and weaving narrow strands
of the leaf blade; the petiole still
serving as a handle to the fan.

Some 1500 species of Palms are
known to science. The species here
pictured is a native of Central
China and is the most common palmate
leafed palm cultivated in our country. The leaves are sometimes as
much as 6 feet across.

The pith of several palms of the
genus Metroxylon of the East Indies
and of some Cycads is used to pre-
pare sago, a starchy food. These
plants while looking like small palms
belong to a different family.

10a Fruit, great globular oblong bodies borne near top of
     trunk. Monoecious. Fig. 20.   COCONUT Cocos nucifera L.

a, tree with nuts; b, cross section of fruit showing nut inside;
c, cross section of germinating
seed.

This is one of the most widely
distributed tropical trees. Its
rather slender trunk attains a
height of 60 to 100 feet. It has
four important uses; the flower
clusters when punctured secrete a
sap from which a beverage "toddy"
is made. Sugar is also made from
this sap. The fruit consists of
a single seed, a coconut, which is
surrounded by a heavy fibrous
covering. The fibers from this
outer husk, "coir," are much used

Figure 20

in the manufacture of mats, brushes, etc.

The coconut, which is the world's largest seed, has a woody
shell lined with about a half-inch layer of white "meat." This
meat and its enclosed liquid ("milk") are important food
sources.

10b Fruit, fleshy cylindric drupes one to two inches long,
     borne in great clusters, arising among the leaves.
     Dioecious. Fig. 21.   DATE PALM Phoenix dactylifera L.

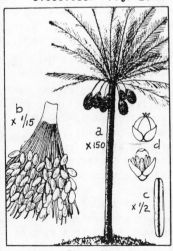

a, tree with bunches of fruit;
b, single spray of fruit; c, seed;
d, flowers.

The use of dried dates for food
goes back many centuries. The
tree seems to have originated in
Africa. It is now rather extensively planted in the near tropical
areas of Texas, Arizona and California. The trees which may reach
a height of 100 feet or more are
distinctly staminate or pistillate.
By practicing hand pollination
only a few staminate trees need to
be grown to insure fruit production of several hundred pistillate
trees. Dates may ripen on the

Figure 21

tree but are usually cut green and ripened in a warm room as
with bananas.

11a Flowers minute, surrounded by
     chaffy bracts (glumes); and
     grouped in spikes or spike-
     lets. Leaves in two rows on
     the stem. Stems usually
     cylindric and almost always
     hollow; fruit a grain.
     Fig. 22. **GRASS FAMILY,** Graminea. 12

Figure 22

11b Plants not as in 11a. . , ... 29

12a Flowers and fruit borne at top of
     plant in spikes (a); or panicles
     (b). 18

12b Staminate flowers borne at top of
     plant in a panicle (tassel); pis-
     tillate flowers and fruit (ear)
     borne in axil of leaves on side
     of plant, enclosed in leafy husks. Fig. 24.

Figure 23

CORN Zea mays L.
(go to number 13 for varieties)

A heavy set solid stemmed, plant normally 3 to 15 feet high.
It is unbranched except that sprouting plants (suckers) often
arise from the base. The lower joints or nodes bear prop or
brace roots which aid in holding the plant erect. The pistillate (female) flowers are borne in spikes arising from the
side of the plant at about half its height. These spikes are
surrounded by a heavy growth of modified leaves, the husks.
Each flower (ovary) develops into a kernel of corn and the
spike becomes an "ear." The flow-
ers or kernels are arranged in
double rows on the cob, so that an
ear of corn may have from 4 to
sometimes more than 20 rows of kernels (but always an even number).

Mature ears range from 3 to 12
inches in length and may contain
800 or more kernels which may be
white, yellow, black, blue or red
and are sometimes striped. Cobs
are either red or white. One
strand of silk arises from each
flower for this is the stigma
which must receive a pollen grain
if the kernel is to mature. The
hundreds of strands of silk run
along the ear and protrude from
the husks at its tip in a mass of
threads.

Figure 24.
"We're from Iowa, Iowa;
   State of all the land;
Joy on every hand
   We're from Iowa, Iowa;
That's where the tall corn grows."

13a The individual kernels of the ear not enclosed in a
pod or husk. 14

13b Each kernel enclosed in a separate pod or husk. **Fig. 25.**

POD CORN _Zea_ _mays_ var. _tunicata_ St. Hil.

a, ear; b, individual kernels.

Pod or Husk Corn as it is some-times called is raised as a novelty rather than for its practical value. All parts of the plant except the ears are the same as in other varie-ties of corn. Each kernel is en-closed separately in a husk, then the entire ear is covered with husks as in other varieties. The kernels may be flint, dent, sweet or pop corn and carry the several corn colors. Pod corn is thought to have been brought to this country from Argentina. It is supposed by some to represent a primitive ancestor of our present day corn.

Figure 25

14a Grains pop when heated (starch grains suddenly expand
turning the kernels inside out). **Fig. 26.**

POP CORN _Zea_ _mays_ var. **_everta_** Bailey.

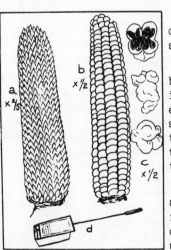

a, rice popcorn; b, pearl pop-corn; c, kernels when "popped"; d, a simple corn popper.

No baseball game or circus could be a success without popcorn. Its importance as a food item is great-er than often realized. The endo-sperm of the kernels is flinty throughout or nearly so. The mois-ture within the kernels causes them to explode when heated.

The small kernels of Rice popcorn are sharp pointed. This type is a favorite for home use. The kernels of Pearl popcorn are smooth and us-ually larger than the rice type. Popcorn has smaller stalks and ears

Figure 26

than field corn. Red, yellow, white and blue colors prevail; occasionally all of these colors appearing in one ear. Ears range from 2 to 7 inches long.

14b Grains not popping when heated. 15

15a Kernels with no corneous (horny starch) endosperm. Grains soft. Fig. 27. SOFT CORN Zea mays var. amylacea Bailey.

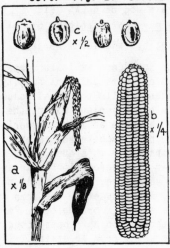

a, stalk with ear; b, typical ear, husked; c, kernels.

Soft corn is much the opposite of Pop corn. In the latter all of the endosperm is hard flinty (corneous) starch whereas in Soft Corn there is no corneous tissue. The kernels maintain their smooth outer surface and resemble Flint Corn. Ears are usually 8 to 10 inches long with 8 to 12 rows of kernels. In general appearance they resemble Flint Corn. It may take any of the corn colors except deep yellow, as corneous tissue is necessary for that color.

Figure 27

The ears of corn found in South American tombs are of this variety. It is planted in South America, Mexico and our Southwestern States and is used in flour making.

15b At least a part of the endosperm of kernels, corneous. .16

16a Kernels horny and translucent throughout; more or less wrinkled. Fig. 28. SWEET CORN Zea mays var. rugosa Bonaf.

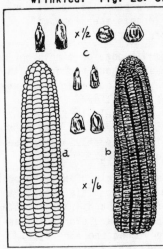

a, ear ready for eating; b, dry ear; c, matured dry kernels.

The leaves and green stems of the corn plants make carbohydrates by photosynthesis. This organized food is transferred through the vascular bundles of the plant in the form of sugar (glucose). When it is stored as in the kernels it is converted into starch, since that is more stable. In sweet corn this change is but partial so that while some starch is found in the kernels, much of the contents is glucose giving it its sweet taste. The fresh unripened kernels

Figure 28

are tightly filled and smooth, but due to shrinkage as the water dries out of the glucose the ripened kernels are much wrinkled. They are also translucent.

Sweet corn is an important food crop, sold fresh from the field or canned in great quantities.

24

16b Kernels smooth; at least at their sides. 17
17a Starchy endosperm wholly enclosed by corneous endosperm;
     kernels small and smooth at end. Fig. 29.

FLINT CORN Zea mays var. indurata Bailey.

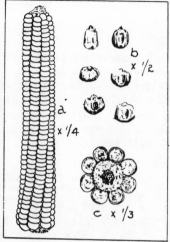

a, typical ear; b, kernels;
c, cross section of ear showing cob
with pith at center.

Flint corn, in character, stands
midway between popcorn and dent
corn. The ears are usually 8 to 15
inches long and comparatively slim
and run to all the common colors of
corn. It has a deeper shade of yellow than found in dent corn. The
number of rows is smaller than in
dent corn, - 4 to 12.

It often produces several ears
to a stalk and is a fairly good
yielder. Columbus found a flint
corn in the West Indies which has
developed into the "tropical flint"

Figure 29

and is now planted in Argentina and some European countries.

17b Kernels with starchy endosperm at top, resulting in a
     characteristic dent when dry. Fig. 30.

DENT CORN Zea mays var. indentata Bailey.

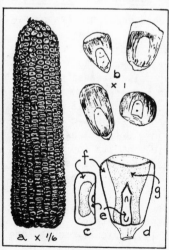

a, typical ear; b, kernels of
different shapes; c, cross section
of kernel; d, longitudinal section
of kernel; e, embryo; f, flinty
starch of endosperm; g, soft starch
of endosperm.

This is the type of corn raised
in the great corn belt of our country. Yellow is the most frequent
color, though white varieties are
common. Red and blue kernels are
sometimes seen.

The practice of crossing two
carefully selected inbred strains
to produce hybrid seed has greatly
increased the corn yield as well
as making the plants much more

Figure 30

uniform. Yields of well over 100 bushels per acre are now common. The average yield for all of Iowa in 1942 was 62 bushels
per acre, the best record yet made in so large an area.

18a Stems hollow; except at the nodes. 22
18b Stems solid. 19
19a Coarse branching plant with imperfect flowers and bearing
hard oval shining seeds about 1/3 inch in diameter.
Fig. 31.   JOB'S TEARS Coix lacryma-jobi L.

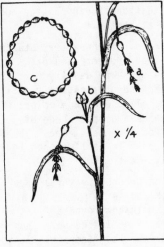

Figure 31

a, staminate flowers; b, seeds;
c, a necklace made of Job's Tears.

This very interesting plant is
thought by some to be an ancestor of
our common corn but efforts to cross
the two have been unsuccessful. It
resembles the corn plant in its
growth habits. It may attain a
height of eight feet.

The smooth enamel-like bluish
seeds are employed as ornaments and
strung for beads or bracelets. A
variety producing soft seeds is
raised in the warmer parts of Asia
for food. In our country it is only
a garden curiosity. It is apparently a native of India.

19b Nodes numerous (several to each foot of stem). Seed seldom produced except in tropics. Fig. 32.

SUGAR-CANE Saccharum officinarum L.

Figure 32

Sugar cane seems to have originated in Arabia. It has a long
history and is raised throughout
the warmer areas of the world. It
is a heavy solid stemmed plant with
the joints closer placed than in
corn. It stands 8 to 15 feet high
with numerous leaves two inches
wide and some 3 feet long. The
silky panicle at its top may be 2
feet in height. It seldom matures
seed and is propogated by planting
pieces of the stem. The making of
sugar from this plant is one of
man's oldest industries. It is
now a highly intricate process and
the investments in raising, harvesting, and processing the plants
makes it one of the world's great industries.

19c Some or all of the flowers perfect. The SORGHUMS. . . . 20

20a Pith with abundant very sweet juice; internodes long;
seeds reddish-brown. Fig. 33.

SWEET SORGHUM Holcus sorghum var. saccharatus Bailey.

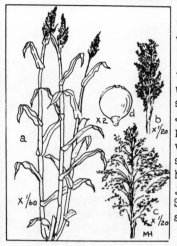

Figure 33

a, growing plant; b, head of
"orange" sorghum; c, head of "amber"
variety; d, seed.

Our present day sorghums are
thought to have been derived from a
widely scattered tropical plant
sometimes raised for forage as
Johnson-grass. The cultural im-
provements of the plant have di-
verged into sweet sorghums and grain
sorghums. The variety saccharatus,
here pictured, has an abundant sweet
juice in its pithy stem from which
Sorghum sirup is made. The plant
attains a height of 8 to 15 feet.

When the plants have reached
their maximum size and the seed is
in the dough stage the quantity of juice and percentage of
sugar are at their best. The leaves are stripped from the
stalks which are then cut and the heads removed. At the mill,
rollers remove the juice which is boiled down. An acre may
produce 200 to 450 gallons of sirup.

20b Pith with but scanty juice; but slightly sweet or somewhat
acid; internodes short; heads cylindrical. Fig. 34.

KAFIR Holcus sorghum var. caffrorum Bailey.

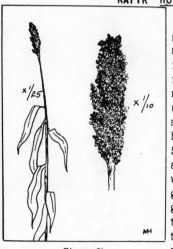

Figure 34

The grain sorghums produce a
grain similar in food value to
maize and can be successfully grown
in semi-arid regions where the rainfall is insufficient for growing
maize. The Kaffirs comprise a valuable group though they run into
several strains or varieties. The
heads are always erect, on plants
5 to 7 feet high. Red, white, pink
and blackhull types are recognized,
with the red seeming to enjoy the
greatest favor. Kaffir came originally from Natal. It is known
that the sorghums have been cultivated in both Africa and Asia for
at least 2000 to 3000 years.

20c Pith dry. 21

21a Fruiting head compact; 4 to 10 inches long; seeds strong-
     ly flattened. Fig. 35.

DURRA <u>Holcus</u> <u>sorghum</u> var. <u>durra</u> Bailey.

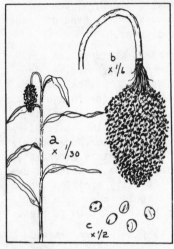

Figure 35

a, mature plant; b, fruiting
head; c, grains.

The stems are medium to heavy, 4
to 7 feet high and ½ to 1½ inches
thick; the pith is usually dry although in some varieties it has
scanty juice. The panicles (fruiting heads) are compact and often
hanging on a recurved stem. The
seeds are decidedly flattened. The
types are separated by their seed
and glume colors.

In our country, Durra is raised
mostly in the Southwest, having
come from Northern Africa. Other
varieties are raised in Northeast
Africa and in India but neither of
these have proven suited to our climate.

21b Head umbel-shaped, the branches much elongated, their tips
     drooping; rachis short, seeds reddish. Fig. 36.

BROOM CORN <u>Holcus</u> <u>sorghum</u> var. <u>technicus</u> Bailey.

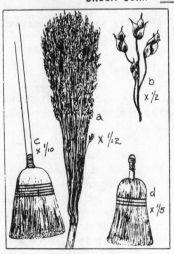

Figure 36

a, part of fruiting head;
b, fruit (seeds); c, broom;
d, whisk broom.

Technically, we neither eat nor
wear broom corn but the variety is
included because of its close relation to food-giving sorghums; and
then the porter brushes us off with
it and that rather vitally relates
it to our wearing apparel. This
plant has been bred to produce long
brush-like panicles with tough,
slender branches.

The plants range up to 15 feet
in height and bear panicles 10 to
28 inches long. The "dwarf" variety is used for whisk brooms and
the like, while the "standard" variety supplies the long fibers.
It is planted and raised about the same as corn.

22a Fruit (seeds) much rounded, often nearly spherical, 1/16 to 1/8 inch in diameter. Figs. 37 to 39. The MILLETS. . 23

22b Fruit larger and elongated. Figs. 40 to 44. The CEREALS 25

23a Head a drooping panicle without awns; 2½ to 4 feet high. Fig. 37. BROOM-CORN MILLET _Panicum miliaceum_ L.

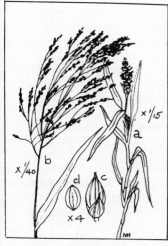

Figure 37

a, plant to show growth habits; b, panicle; c, spiklet bearing one seed; d, seed.

This is the true millet of the old world which has been cultivated for its seed to use as food since before our earliest history. It does well in poor soil and with scant rainfall. It is an annual attaining a height of 3 to 4 feet. Its stems and leaves are rather densely covered with hairs. The seeds are ground for flour and may be used in puddings and soups. It often plays an important role in canary bird seed. It is a good short season plant and has been extensively raised in our northern areas.

23b Inflorescence a spike (sometimes compounded) with numerous bristles or awns. 24

24a Globose grain opening the hull at maturity. Spike dense. Plants 3 to 8 feet tall; stems pithy. Fig. 38.

PEARL MILLET _Pennisetum glaucum_ R. Br.

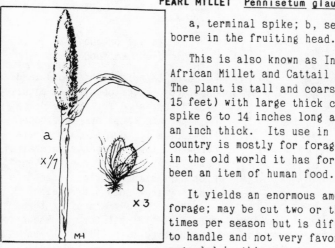

Figure 38

a, terminal spike; b, seed as borne in the fruiting head.

This is also known as Indian or African Millet and Cattail Millet. The plant is tall and coarse (6 to 15 feet) with large thick compact spike 6 to 14 inches long and often an inch thick. Its use in this country is mostly for forage but in the old world it has for ages been an item of human food.

It yields an enormous amount of forage; may be cut two or three times per season but is difficult to handle and not very favorably regarded in this country.

24b Seed enclosed in hull when mature; spike rather open.
     Plants 2 to 5 feet tall. Fig. 39.

FOXTAIL MILLETS <u>Setaria italica</u> Beauv.

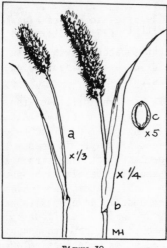

Figure 39

a, Hungarian millet; b, Common millet; c, seed.

When Millet is mentioned in America it is usually this plant that is in mind. It is an annual, growing from 2 to 5 feet high. The head is a compact cylindrical panicle with many short awns and very numerous nearly spherical seeds. The seeds are usually yellow but other colors are found in some varieties. This plant is highly prolific. The seeds are used as human food in the Old World, but with us this species of millet figures largely as a forage plant and for cropping purposes.

25a Inflorescence a panicle (as in Fig. 41). 26
25b Inflorescence a spike (as in Fig. 42). 27
26a Spikelets flattened and but one seeded. Fig. 40.

RICE <u>Oryza sativa</u> L.

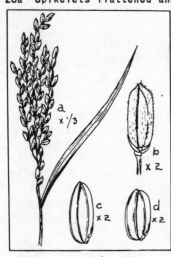

Figure 40

a, fruiting head; b, spikelet with one seed; c, grain of long Hondurus type; d, grain of Japanese type.

This in all probability is the world's greatest food plant.

Rice is normally a flood-land crop but in our country is usually sowed and cared for as the other small grain crops but is flooded by irrigation during part of its growth, then the water is drained away and binders or combines used for harvesting. Upland rice is a variety that does not require flooding. The grain after threshing is still enclosed in its hull and in this form is known as "paddy rice." When the hull is removed by milling, "brown rice" results; further milling removes this coat and the grains are then put through a polishing process which yields rice as we ordinarily know it.

26b Spiklets rounded and usually producing two or three seeds (rarely but one). Fig. 41.   OATS _Avena sativa_ L.

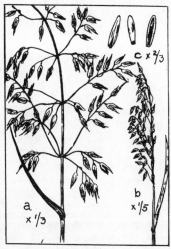

Figure 41

a, head of spreading oats; b, head of side-oats; c, threshed grains.

This is a highly important food crop. The plants grow 2 to 4 feet high. There are two types, spreading oats and side-oats, the former being the one most frequently raised. It is a self-pollinated plant which makes improvement fairly easy to attain and retain. There are many recent varieties which have greatly raised the average yield.

Oats (with the exception of "Naked Oats") like barley and rice retains its hull when threshed and makes it lighter in weight than wheat or rye.

Wild oats, whether the weed species, _Avena fatua_, or the kind purportedly sown by ill-advised young folks have no food value.

27a Each node of rachis bearing 3 one-flowered spikelets. Grain retains its hull when threshed. Fig. 42.

BARLEY _Hordeum vulgare_ L.

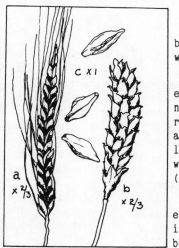

Figure 42

a, head of bearded barley; b, beardless variety: c, grains when threshed.

This is thought to be man's oldest grain crop. It likely originated in Western Asia. The plant resembles wheat but does not grow as tall. The actual kernel is much like that of wheat but is covered with the flowering glume and palea (floral parts) which make the hull.

Barley will thrive in even colder climates than wheat or rye. It is a favorite for making malt beverages. Barley meal is much used for baking in Europe but lacks favor in America. Pearl barley is made by removing the hull and polishing the grains. It is used as a cereal and in soups.

31

27b Each node of rachis bearing but one spikelet which
matches two or more grains. **28**

28a Spikelets uniformly 3-flowered producing 2 grains with
the middle flower sterile. Glumes one-nerved and nar-
row. Fig. 43.   RYE **Secale cereale** L.

Figure 43

a, typical head; b, threshed
grains; c, head with two Ergoted
grains - a common fungus disease of
rye.

Rye resembles wheat but is a
taller plant and will grow in a
colder climate. It is the principal grain crop of Northern Europe
and parts of Asia. It has been
known for some 2000 years but not
as long as wheat and rye. Since
it is cross-pollinated there are
comparatively few varieties. Like
all the small grains, stooling or
tillering greatly multiplies the
yield. When a seed grain grows it
does not produce just one stalk as
might be supposed, but sends up several stalks each bearing a
fruiting head.

28b Spikelets with 2 to 5 flowers. Glumes broader and with 3
nerves. Fig. 44.   WHEAT **Triticum aestivum** L.

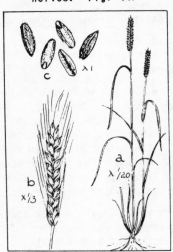

Figure 44

a, typical plant of beardless
wheat; b, head of bearded wheat;
c, wheat grains.

Wheat is a close rival to rice
as the world's greatest food plant.
It is an annual grass easily
raised and growing in many parts
of the world. The grains will
average a bit shorter and notice-
ably plumper than rye. In some
regions it is sowed in the fall
and makes considerable growth before cold weather, rests during
the winter then completes its
growth the following year.

Spring wheat is not sowed till
after winter and makes its entire
growth in the one season. Fall wheat is usually the harder
grain and makes the best flour. Wheat flour is superior to
all others for bread-making due to its quantities of gluten.

29a Broad-leaved tropical plants with flowers borne on a fleshy
     spadix surrounded by a spathe (as in Calla Lily). . . . 30

29b Not as in 29a 31

30a Plant without stem above ground. Edible parts the heavy
     corms from which the broad "elephant ear" leaves arise.
     Fig. 45.   DASHEEN Colocasia esculenta Schott.

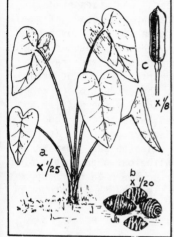

a, plant; b, the corms; c, flowers.

This very large-leaved plant is confined to regions of warm climate. The plant grows from a central large corm weighing up to 6 pounds and produces numerous smaller lateral tubers about the size of a hen egg or larger. The outer covering is fibrous and brown, the interior is white and starchy. These corms can be prepared for the table the same way as potatoes and make a good substitute. They have less water than potatoes. They have a pleasing nutty flavor.

Figure 45

Young forced blanched shoots from the corms are eaten similarly to asparagus. In Hawaii and other Pacific islands this plant is known as Taro and has been much prized by the natives. Another name is "Eddo."

30b A climbing plant with large thick perforated leaves.
     Edible part the large spadix which ripens into a fleshy
     fruit. Fig. 46.   CERIMAN Monstera delicosa Liebm.

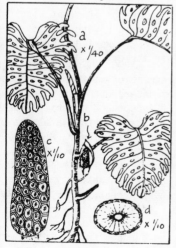

a, portion of plant; b, spathe (a bract) surrounding the spadix of the inflorescence; c, mature fruit; d, cross section through fruit.

This tropical American woody climber may be distinguished by its large thick leaves up to 3 feet across and which are perforated with numerous large slots and holes. The flowering spathe attains a length of 10 to 16 inches and is nearly white. It surrounds the fleshy somewhat shorter spadix which in this plant, becomes edible when ripened. The thin outer yellowish-green covering peels off readily.

Figure 46

33

31a Plants with great stiff fleshy leaves in basal rosettes. The leaves are usually spiny especially at the tip. Fig. 47. AGAVES Agave spp.

Figure 47

The genus is made up of about 300 species of plants. In Mexico and other tropical lands, Agaves furnish fibers, food, fermented liquors and soap. The bases of the fleshy leaves and the flower buds are eaten. Sisal, Henequen, Maguey, Ixtle, and other fibers are made from these plants, most of which goes into the production of ropes and cords as they are usually too coarse and harsh to make good cloth. The Century Plant (several species) which we see grown as an ornamental belong here. They bloom in ten or so years in the tropics at which time the food contents of the great fleshy leaves is consumed in building the stately flowering panicle sometimes 40 feet high and bearing hundreds of flowers.

31b Plants not as in 31a. **32**
32a Edible part the fruit **33**
32b Underground parts or leaves used for food **34**
32c Thick young stems used for food. Older plants, tall, much divided with small yellow lily-like flowers and spherical fruit (red when ripe). Fig. 48.
  GARDEN ASPARAGUS Asparagus officinalis L.

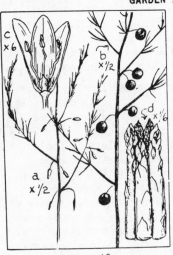

Figure 48

a, small branch of plant with flowers; b, branch with fruit; c, section of flower; d, "spears" as cut for market.

Asparagus over-winters as a mass of fleshy underground stems (rhizomes) at a depth of several inches. The mature plants attain a height of 5 to 6 feet. The flowers are tiny, hanging and tulip-shaped. Their color is yellow. The fruit is a berry, scarlet at maturity. The fleshy young sprouts or "spears" are cut close to the ground when they have attained a height of 4 to 8 inches and bunched for marketing or canning.

34

33a Edible part a collective fruit (many ovaries united to
form a single fruit); leaves heavy, sword-like, spiny.
Fig. 49.   PINEAPPLE Ananas comosus Marr.

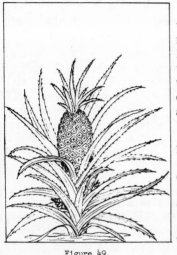

Figure 49

The pineapple is a native of
tropical South America, but is now
raised most largely in Cuba and
Porto Rico, which supply most of
the fresh fruit, and in Hawaii
which produces 75% of the world's
crop and features canned pineapple
and pineapple juice.

When the "pine" is young, small
purplish-blue flowers appear, one
in each eye of the cone. From
each flower a berry develops, all
packed closely together into a
collective fruit.

The leaves yield a fiber from
which the beautiful Philippine
"pina" cloth is made.

33b Edible part the elongated fruit borne in large bunches.
Fig. 50.   BANANA Musa paradisica var. sapientum L.

Figure 50

a, plant bearing a bunch of
fruit; b, the flower bracts and
young fruit; c, ripe banana.

The Banana is a native of the
East Indies now grown in tropical
America. This species may attain
a trunk diameter of a foot or
more and a height of 30 feet,
with leaves 2 feet wide and 9
feet long. After bearing a bunch
of bananas the main shoot dies
but is replaced by suckers which
have grown up around it. The
flowers are borne in clusters or
"hands" of 8 to 15. Each of the
7 to 15 hands on the main stem
are at first covered by a broad,
usually purplish-red scale.

No other agricultural crop can produce as large yields
per acre as the banana. The Abaca (Musa textilis) has been a
highly important fiber plant of the Philippines and the East
Indies for cloth and cordage.

33c Flavoring extract made from fleshy bean-shaped pods.
Rather fleshy climbing vine with thick leaves and fairly
large flowers. Fig. 51.

COMMON VANILLA <u>Vanilla planifolia</u> Andr.

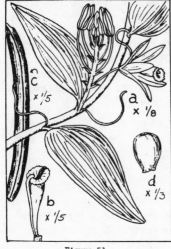

Figure 51

a, part of vine; b, "column" of
flower; c, fruit pod; d, seed.

This climbing vine is an orchid.
Its commercial worth lies in the
"beans" from which vanilla extract
is prepared. The flowers are
greenish-yellow with lavender markings and about four inches across;
the leaves attain a length of 8
inches. The pods are from 6 to 10
inches long and from $\frac{1}{2}$ to $\frac{3}{4}$ inch
thick.

Vanilla is a native American
plant and was utilized for flavoring before the discovery of the
continent. Southern Mexico produces the best vanilla though it
is raised in both the West and East Indies.

34a Lily-like plants growing from true bulbs. Usually the
bulbs are eaten, but sometimes the leaves. 35

34b Food source the more or less thickened true roots or
rhizomes 40

35a Leaves cylindrical and hollow. 37

35b Leaves solid and grasslike 36

36a Leaves broad. Fig. 52.   LEEK <u>Allium porrum</u> L.

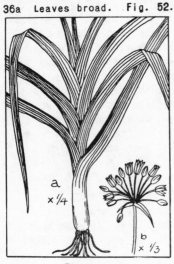

Figure 52

a, plant as eaten; b, flowering
head.

This is a close relative of the
common onion. Its slender elongated bulb is eaten as are also
the leaves. The flavor when
cooked is milder than that of the
onion and distinctive. It is
often used in soups. The flowers
are pinkish. The plants may attain a height of 3 feet with
leaves 2 inches broad. The plants
are hardy and can live outside
during the winter; for convenience
of winter use they are usually
stored in the cellar in early
winter.

36b Leaves narrow; bulbs composed of many bulbils. Fig. 53

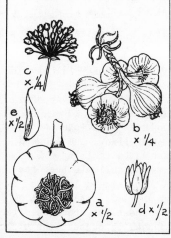

Figure 53

GARLIC **Allium sativum** L.

a, bulb; b, bulbs as frequently tied for winter; c, umbel of flowers; d, single flower; e, a "clove."

Garlic is a favorite European plant of the onion group. Its pinkish flowers grow in dense umbels on long stalks. The flowers are often intermingled with small bulbils which may be planted to raise a new crop. The plant may reach 2 feet in height. It is raised for its bulbs which are made up of 8 to 15 sections known as "cloves," separated from each other by dry scales. Seed seldom matures and the cloves are the usual means of propagation.

A closely related Wild Garlic often grows in fields and if eaten by dairy cattle gives an objectionable taste to their milk.

37a Bulbs very small growing in dense clumps; leaves used for seasoning; flowers rose-colored, prominent. Fig. 54.

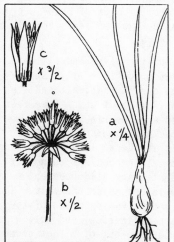

Figure 54

CHIVE **Allium schoenoprasum** L.

a, single plant; b, umbel of flowers; c, a single flower.

Chives are very hardy and once started will usually perpetuate themselves. The plants when left to themselves grow in thick masses which need to be divided and reset from time to time. They are frequently raised for ornament as the rose-purple flowers are fairly attractive, and make good border plants.

The bulbs are poorly formed so the leaves are the parts used for food in soups, salads and stews. The plants produce seed readily which permits easy large-scale raising. It is thought to be of European or Asiatic origin. Another form of the word is "Cive."

37

37b Bulbs larger; not in dense clumps. **38**
38a Bulbs clustered; leaves awl-shaped, short. Fig. 55.

SHALLOT Allium ascalonicum L.

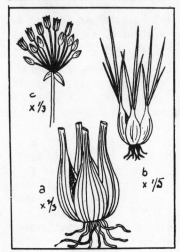

Figure 55

a, bulbs; b, growing plants;
c, flowering head.

This plant likely originated in
Asia. Its base is divided into several somewhat angular bulbs which
are attached at their lower end.
The leaves are short (one foot or
less) and awl-like. The flowers
shade from white to lilac. The
flavor is more delicate than that
of onions; it is used in stews,
soups and pickles. Shallots are
used while fresh but are more often
dried and used throughout the winter
Small red onions are sometimes seen
in the market, being sold as shallot

38b Leaves longer; bulbs not in clusters. 3
39a Bulb well developed. Fig. 56. COMMON ONION Allium cepa L

Figure 56

a, bulb and leaves; b, a mature
bulb (there are many shapes) c, umbe
of flowers; d, stem of bulb in cross
section; e, swollen leaf (scale) for
food storage.

Do you like liver and lilies?
Well, the onion is a lily, and a
fragrant one at that. It and its
"cousins," five of which have been
pictured and described, belong to
the genus Allium and to the Lily
family. The genus is a rather large
one, containing besides these six
food plants many wild ones and a few
species valued as ornamentals. The
leaves and flowering stems of the
Onion are cylindrical and hollow and
may reach a height of 3 feet or more

A variety known as "Top Onions" produce little bulbils instead
of flowers on the fruiting stalk. These are saved and set out.
The onion sets commonly bought in the spring are just small
bulbs that have been grown from seed the preceding year.

Field onions may yield as high as 600 bushels per acre.

39b Bulb but poorly developed at maturity. **Fig. 57.**

WELSH ONION Allium fistulosum L.

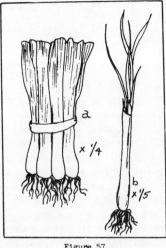

Figure 57

a, bunched for market; b, a plant as it grows.

This is another Asiatic onion which has a bulb but slightly thicker than its neck. The bulb is softer than other onions. The flowers are in dense umbels and are white with long protruding stamens. It is grown from seed.

The flavor is mild; the leaves are used for seasoning. Other names are Ciboule, Spring Onion and Rock Onion.

40a Herbaceous vines, bearing large fleshy roots and winged seeds. **Fig. 58.** **CHINESE YAM** Dioscorea batatas Decne.

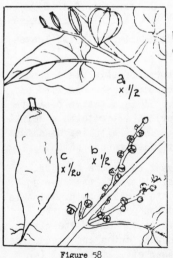

Figure 58

a, female vine with fruit; b, staminate vine with flowers; c, a root.

The term "Yam" is often erroneously applied to large sweet potatoes (Ipomoea batatus), which see. The true Yams are mostly tropical or belonging to the near-tropics where they are extensively used for food. The plants are strong climbing vines, of several similar species. The tuberous-like roots attain great size often weighing 30 pounds and more rarely even 100 pounds. The roots are of high food value.

Among other species than the one shown here are the YELLOW or ATTOTO YAM of the West Indies and Brazil, the CUSH-CUSH or YAMPEE - a South American species with smaller tubers and the AIR POTATO (Dioscorea bulbifera) which bears tubers on the vine. These may attain a length of a foot and weigh several pounds. They are edible and nutritious.

40b   Food derived from rhizomes (fleshy underground stems). . 41
41a   Rhizomes very irregular; above ground stems unbranched,
       leafy, 2 to 4 feet high. Fig. 59.

COMMON GINGER Zingiber officinale Roscoe.

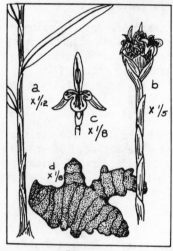

Figure 59

a, stalk with leaves; b, flowering spike; c, a flower; d, rhizome.

This native of the East India islands grows from a perennial root system, but the top dies down annually. It is widely cultivated throughout the tropics. It grows to a height of 3 feet. The flowers are bright yellow marked with purple and in shape resemble some of the orchids. The rhizomes are used by cleaning and scraping to produce the ginger of the market. Young growing roots are cut into sections, boiled and cured in syrup, and put into jars as a confection.

Ginger-ale, Jamaica ginger and ginger-tea are other products of this plant.

41b   Rhizomes more regular. Stems much branched, 2 to 6 feet
       high. Fig. 60.

ARROWROOT Maranta arundinacea L.

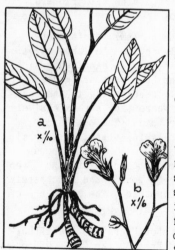

Figure 60

a, plant with roots and leaves; b, flowers.

The roots of this plant furnish arrowroot starch and one kind of tapioca. It is a native of tropical America. It attains a height of 5 or 6 feet, with leaves a foot long; its flowers are white.

The year old roots are dug, thoroughly cleaned, then beaten and rasped into a milky pulp, which is strained and put away for the starch to settle out. The starch is thoroughly dried and then canned for the market. It is used for desserts and in cooking especially for invalids and children because it is highly digestible.

DICOTYLEDONS

42a Plants used by man for his food. 43

42b Plants we wear 239

43a Flowers with 4 separated similar petals, fruit a
     silique (pod with thin partition through center and ½
     the seeds on each side). Food parts, - roots, stems,
     leaves, flowers or seed. A very important food pro-
     ducing family. Figs. 61-77. MUSTARD FAMILY 44

43b Flowers and fruit not as in 43a. 59

44a Stem above ground thickened into a fleshy edible part.
     Fig. 61.   KOHLRABI _Brassica caulorapa_ Pasq.

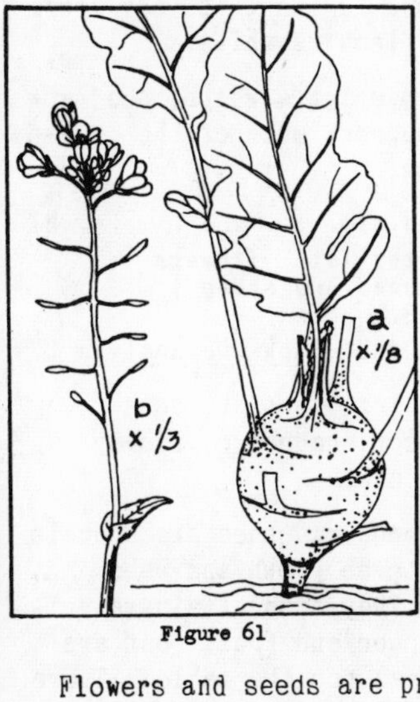

Figure 61

a, growing plant; b, flower and fruit stalk.

This plant resembles a turnip which forgot to keep its fleshy part under ground. It is the stem rather than the root which serves as a storage organ. In flavor it resembles the turnip but is milder.

The plant grows to a height of 10 to 18 inches; the edible tuber is usually 2 to 4 inches in diameter and often purplish-red. The names "Stem-turnip" and "Turnip-Rooted Cabbage" are sometimes given it.

It should be grown quickly and eaten while young. It has the same insect pests as cabbage.

Flowers and seeds are produced the second year on old stocks. They are similar to those of cabbage.

44b Not as in 44a. 45

45a Thickened fleshy roots used for food 46

45b Not as in 45a. 49

46a Perennial plant with long irregular somewhat woody roots.
Roots grated or ground for use in relishes or condiments;
too hot to be eaten directly. Fig. 62.

HORSE-RADISH Armoracia rusticana Gaertn.

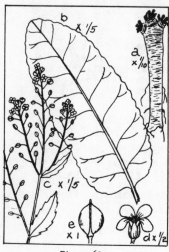

Figure 62

a, root as ready for the market;
b, a typical leaf; c, flower and
fruit branch; d, single flower;
e, mature fruit.

This perennial, which reaches a
height of 2 to 3 feet, is a native
of Europe but is frequently found
growing spontaneously as an escape.
Where it is grown commercially a
yield of five tons or more per
acre may be had. The small lateral roots which are trimmed away
before marketing the main roots,
are planted to start the new crop.
The root flesh is white.

The flowers are white, and appear throughout much of the growing season.

46b Roots eaten raw or cooked as food. 47
47a Plants annuals; biennial if planted late, flowers
white or rose-lilac; fruit thickened and spongy,
indehiscent, few seeded. Fig. 63.

GARDEN RADISH Raphanus sativus L.

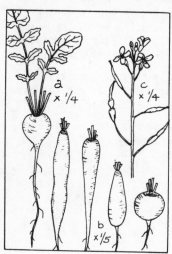
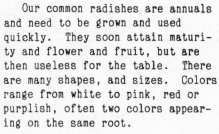

Figure 63

a, growing plant; b, some
typical root shapes; c, flower
and fruit stalk

Our common radishes are annuals
and need to be grown and used
quickly. They soon attain maturity and flower and fruit, but are
then useless for the table. There
are many shapes, and sizes. Colors
range from white to pink, red or
purplish, often two colors appearing on the same root.

"Summer" and "Winter radishes,"
both large biennials, and the "Rat-
tail radish" the foot long pods of
which are eaten instead of its slim
root, all belong to this same
species.

47b Biennials, flowers yellow, fruit long, many seeded
     (15-25), dehiscent. 48

48a Leaves arising from top of swollen root; flesh white
     or whitish. Fig. 64.   TURNIP Brassica rapa L.

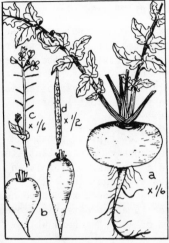

a, typical turnip; b, other root shapes; c, flower and fruit stalk; d, mature fruit (silique).

Turnips produce fairly large underground fleshy taproots of various shapes but usually flattened. The flesh is white and fairly fine grained. The roots are whitish with their upper parts tinged with reddish-purple. They may attain a weight of 40 pounds but are usually much smaller and only a few inches in diameter.

The roots when kept through the winter and then planted out, quickly produce flowers, fruit and seeds.

Figure 64

48b Swollen root with short stem or neck at top from which
     leaves arise; flesh yellow or orange. Fig. 65.
                    RUTABAGA Brassica napobrassica Mill.

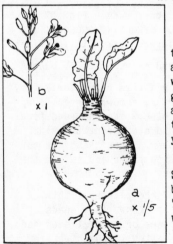

a, root and leaves; b, flowers.

The leaves of this plant grow to a length of 12 to 24 inches and are moderately covered with a whitish bloom giving them a blue-green shade. The plant is hardier and slower growing than its sister, the Turnip. The flowers are bright yellow and about 3/8 inch across.

Rutabagas are known also as Swede Turnips or "Swedes" and are best when grown in a cool climate. They average a few pounds in weight but may become much larger.

Figure 65

49a The inflorescence with young buds or flowers used for
     food. 50

49b Not as in 49a 51

50a Plant with large compact head of aborted flowers or thickened stems. Head surrounded and overtopped by cabbage-like leaves; head whitish. Fig. 66.

CAULIFLOWER <u>Brassica</u> <u>oleracea</u> var. <u>botrytis</u> L.

a, top view of head.

This is one of several varieties of plants thought to have sprung from a wild mustard growing on the shores of western Europe. This <u>Brassica oleracea</u> in all of its varieties is one of the world's most important vegetables.

The Cauliflower plant grows and looks like cabbage, except that its head is a great mass of fasciated flowering stalks and buds. The leaves grow up around this head and in field culture are often tied over it to make or keep the head white.

Figure 66

True Broccoli is slower growing but quite similar to Cauliflower. Asparagus or Sprouting Broccoli is the plant many know as Broccoli.

50b Heads more open and rising above the surrounding leaves; usually green with yellowish flower buds. Fig. 67.

ASPARAGUS or SPROUTING BROCCOLI
<u>Brassica</u> <u>oleracea</u> var. <u>italica</u> Plenck.

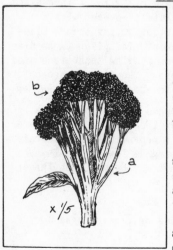

a, head or panicle; b, buds.

This plant is characterized by its aborted, somewhat-open flowering panicles. The buds and flowers are more apparent than in cauliflower. This "head" is cut while quite green and before the buds open.

All of the plants of this species are grown from seeds in green houses or special seed beds and when a few inches high are transplanted to field or garden. They are biennials and when kept alive into the second year produce flowers and seed. The production of vegetable seeds is a specialized business. The seeds of these cabbage-like plants are largely grown in California.

Figure 67

51a Both seeds and leaves used for food. 52
51b Leaves of plants (sometimes in compact heads) used for food 53
52a Fruit (pods) ½ to 1 inch long; held close to stem when ripe, seeds dark colored; stem leaves usually hairy. Fig. 68.   **BLACK MUSTARD** Brassica nigra Koch.

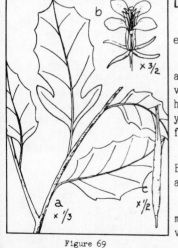

a, flowers and fruit on branch; b, fruit (silique).

This is a much branched annual, usually with stiff hairs. It grows to a height of 3 to 10 ft. The flowers are small and bright yellow. The fruit is short, usually less than one inch and very abundant.

The basal leaves of young plants are used for greens. The seeds are ground to make table mustard.

This plant is of European origin but has been scattered world-wide and is a bad weed, often growing abundantly in small grain fields and other places where it is not wanted.

Figure 68

52b Fruit 1½ to 2½ inches long, spreading when ripe: seeds yellow, stem and leaves often smooth. Fig. 69.

LEAF MUSTARD Brassica juncea Cass.

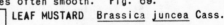

a, branch with leaves; b, flowers; c, fruit.

There are several mustard plants and weeds all of which are rather variable. This species grows to a height of 2 to 4 feet, has bright yellow flowers and rather large fruit pods.

It is of Asiatic origin and like Black Mustard is used for greens, and the seed for table mustard.

It is sometimes known as Chinese mustard. There is a curled leaf variety.

Figure 69

53a Leaves closely appressed forming one or more heads. . . 54
53b Leaves not forming heads. 55

54a One single large somewhat-spherical head terminating the
stem, surrounded by the earlier leaves. **Fig. 70.**

CABBAGE Brassica oleracea var. capitata L.

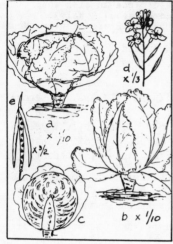

a & b, cabbage heads of two common types; c, longitudinal section through head; d, flowers; e, fruit.

Next to potatoes, cabbage is likely the most largely used vegetable. It supplies the much needed minerals, vitamins and bulk at a minimum of cost.

The plant has stored quantities of foods in the head to provide for quick growth of the flowering and fruiting parts, early the second season. Man comes in and uses these foods stored in the compactly grown fleshy leaves for his own use.

Figure 70

Cabbage does best when the weather is cool. There are many strains and varieties of shape and color. In Savoy cabbage the leaves are much wrinkled and blistered.

54b One single large cylindrical head terminating the stem.
Fig. 71.

PE-TSAI or CHINESE CABBAGE Brassica pekinensis Rupr.

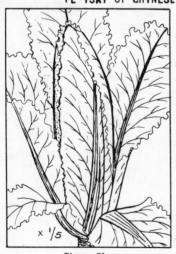

Chinese or "celery cabbage" is an old Chinese food plant now widely used in our country. It has a milder flavor than cabbage and is a favorite for salads and greens. The heads are elongate and slim with the inner parts bleached and will average a foot or more in length. The flowers are light yellow and the fruit rather short and heavy.

Other East Asia plants of similar nature are PAK-CHOI (Brassica chinensis L.) and FALSE PAK-CHOI (Brassica parachinensis Bailey) but neither of these are so frequently seen with us. They have less compact heads and find use in salads or as pot-herbs.

Figure 71

46

54c Many smaller heads growing along the side of the stem in
     the axils of the leaves. Fig. 72.

     BRUSSELS SPROUTS Brassica oleracea var. gemmifera Zenker.

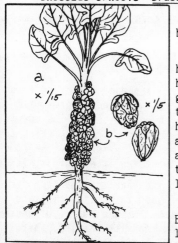

a, plant as grown; b, individual heads.

Scatter a lot of tiny cabbage heads along an erect stem and you have Brussels Sprouts as it is grown. The plants are raised and treated much like cabbage. The heads or "sprouts" are botanically, axillary buds which develop in the axils of the lateral leaves. When the sprouts are partly grown the leaves are removed.

The plant has been grown in Belgium (hence the name) for nearly a thousand years. The flavor is mild and in much favor. An

Figure 72

average plant should produce about a quart of sprouts. The sprouts are ready to pick in the fall and the plant will produce flowers, fruit and seed the second season if kept indoors or protected from severe weather.

55a Fruit dehiscent (splitting open when ripe), used for
     salads, greens, etc. 56
55b Fruit indehiscent, one seeded. Fleshy perennial with
     cabbage-like leaves. Fig. 73.

     SEA-KALE Crambe maritima L.

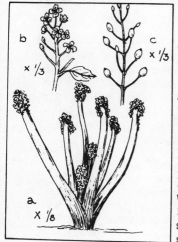

a, shoots as gathered and eaten; b, tip of flowering branch; c, fruit.

This large-leaved plant attains a height of 3 feet and an age of 10 to 12 years. It grows along the west coast of Europe. The leaves are bluish-green and very large, often 2 feet or more in length. They are notched and lobed more than cabbage leaves which they otherwise resemble. It is the fleshy young blanched shoots which are eaten in much the same way as Asparagus. The plants are usually covered with light-

Figure 73

tight receptacles to promote the maximum growth and to blanch the shoots.

47

56a Fruit elongated. **57**

56b Fruit as broad as long. Flowers white, very small.
     Stems and leaves glabrous and glaucous. Fig. 74.

GARDEN CRESS Lepidium sativum L.

Figure 74

a, basal part of plant; b, flowering and fruiting shoot; c, section of flower; d, fruit.

This is a pepper grass, of which several related species grow wild and are sometimes used. Its use is similar to that of parsley which the leaves somewhat resemble. The flowers are white and the fruit winged.

It is an annual raised from seed and does best in early spring and late fall. It is a native of Western Asia. As with parsley, there are curled-leaf varieties which may prove more attractive but taste the same.

57a Rather heavy glabrous plants; flowers yellow. **58**

57b Creeping or floating in water; leaves much cut; flowers
     large, white. Fig. 75.

WATER-CRESS Roripa nasturtium-aquaticum Hayek.

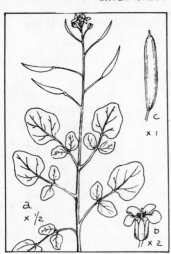

Figure 75

a, branch of plant with flower and fruit; b, flower; c, fruit.

This trailing, prostrate plant grows in cold water or mud, and having been started, usually develops spontaneously. It is valued in salads and for garnishing, not only for its flavor but also because it is very tender and brittle.

Its native home is Europe but is widely scattered because of its hardiness. The flowers are white and the fruit long stemmed. The branches take root readily when put in water or mud.

BITTER-CRESS Cardamine pratensis
L. with white to rose-purple flowers is sometimes similarly used

48

58a Various "headless cabbage" plants. Some varieties have very much curled leaves. Fig. 76.

KALES, BORECOLE Brassica oleracea var. acephala DC.

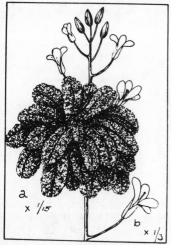

a, typical plant (curled variety); b, flowering branch.

This is one of the "cabbage plants" again, but this variety, - which runs to several strains and uses - has no modified parts. The entire plant is cut for the market although for home use, a few leaves are sometimes removed and the plant left to grow.

Collards, Tree Kales and Cow Kales belong here. They are all biennials. The curled-leaf strains seem to be most highly favored.

Figure 76

58b Dark green, thick growing, early blooming. Often abundant in fields as an escape. Fig. 77.

WINTER-CRESS Barbarea vulgaris R. Br.

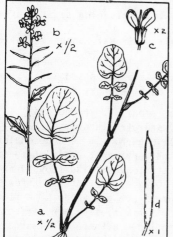

a, branch of plant; b, flowering and fruiting branch; c, flower; d, fruit.

This European plant has become a common roadside and field weed with us. Its quick growth and brilliant yellow flowers makes it conspicuous in early spring. It reaches a height of nearly 2 feet and is often a perennial.

Barbarea verna is also known as Winter-Cress or Upland-Cress. It is somewhat smaller in its growing habits.

Figure 77

Several other members of the mustard family find occasional food uses. The family is a large one, widely distributed and contains many ornamental plants, also. Most of the members of the family have a sharp peppery flavor. It is this that makes the Cresses desirable as salad plants.

59a Fleshy fruit-bearing trees, shrubs and perennial plants with regular 5 petaled flowers, usually showy; stamens numerous, borne on a collar-like ring. See Figs. 81-107. ROSE FAMILY. 60

Figure 78. a, fleshy receptacle with dry achenes on surface; b, longitudinal section of a; c, an aggregation of many druplets.

59b Not as above 81

60a Plants producing aggregate fruits (few, to many fruit units arising from one flower and united into one fruit). Fig. 78. 61

60b Plants producing stone (drupe) fruits (fleshy fruit with single stone covered "seed" near center). Fig. 79 70

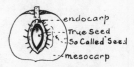

endocarp
True Seed
So Called Seed
mesocarp

Figure 79

60c Plants producing pome fruits (fleshy fruits with five divisioned woody or papery "core" containing the several seeds). Fig. 80. 77

61a Fruit a collection of a few, to many small drupes (each "seed" with a separate flesh and skin covering) shrubs or low vines. 62

Figure 80. a, cross section of pome; b, longitudinal section.

61b Fruit with small hard "seeds" (really achenes) scattered over the surface of a fleshy receptacle; fruit red when ripe. Plants with very short woody stems spreading by elongated runners. Fig. 81.

STRAWBERRY Fragaria chiloensis var. ananassa Bailey

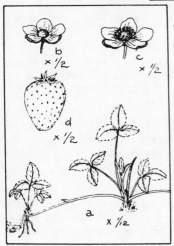

Figure 81

a, small plant with runner; b, flower with few stamens; c, flower with many stamens; d, fruit.

This is one of our choicest fruits, and structurally different from all others. It is a perennial herb with very short woody stems and trifoliate leaves. The flowers are white. On some varieties but few if any stamens are produced. The flowers of other varieties are perfect and have large numbers of stamens. The varieties which produce few stamens must be grown along side of some perfect-flowered variety that blooms at the same time so that pollination may be sufficiently complete to insure a good crop.

The Everbearing strawberries are derived from Fragaria vesca L.

62a When ripe fruit is picked the receptacle remains on the
plant. Fig. 83d. RASPBERRIES. 63

62b When ripe fruit is picked the receptacle is detached
from the plant and is a part of the "berry." BLACK-
BERRIES, etc. 65

63a Flowers small, whitish, about ½ inch across. 64

63b Flowers 1 inch across in groups of 1-4, rose or
purplish; fruit salmon to wine-red. Fig. 82.

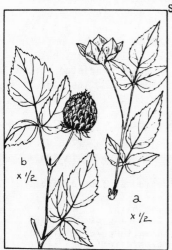

Figure 82

SALMONBERRY **Rubus spectabilis** Pursh.

a, branch with flower; b, with
fruit.

The Salmonberry is a native of
the Rocky Mountain region and while
edible and sometimes planted is not
important as a food plant. It is a
strong growing bush with but few
thorns. The flowers are fully an
inch in diameter and colored with
different shades of rose, making it
an attractive plant. The flowers
are in groups of 1 to 4. The fruit,
½ to ¾ inch in diameter, is salmon
to rose-red.

In flower and fruit (but not in
its foliage) the Salmonberry some-
what resembles the Flowering Raspberry of our eastern mountains.

64a Fruit purplish black when mature; glaucous canes 3-5 feet
high, recurving and taking root at tip thus starting new
plants. Fig. 83. BLACKCAP RASPBERRY **Rubus occidentalis** L.

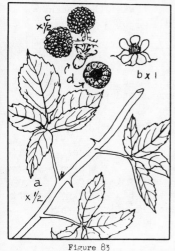

Figure 83

a, stem with leaves and thorns;
b, flower; c, fruit; d, fruit removed with receptacle remaining on
the plant.

This plant, sometimes known as
the Thimble-berry, reaches a height
of 5 or 6 feet, but the much longer "canes" bend over and take root
at their tips, by which means the
plant is propogated. The canes
are purplish-red and thickly
covered in part with a white bloom.
The flowers are greenish-white and
rather inconspicuous.

Many cultivated varieties and
hybrids of raspberries are known.

64b Fruit red when ripe, canes not rooting at tips. Fig. 84.

RED RASPBERRY _Rubus idaeus_ L.

Figure 84

a, stem and leaves; b, flower; c, fruit.

This species is of European origin, though it is now more widely raised and is hardier than our black raspberries. The canes are light colored and do not take root at their tips. Multiplication is by sprouts or suckers arising at the base of the plants. The flowers are small and white. The fruit is larger and softer than that of the black caps. The Purple Raspberries or "Purple-Canes" are hybrids of the Red Raspberry and the Blackcap.

65a Plants prostrate or creeping; rooting at tips or nodes or both. The DEWBERRIES. 66

65b Plants erect or arched, multiplying mainly by suckers though in some cases rooting at tips. The BLACKBERRIES. 69

66a Main stems pruinose (covered with white powdery bloom); at first ascending but becoming prostrate; stems circular in cross section with thorns scattered. 67

66b Main stems without bloom; seldom at all ascending; stems angled with most of the thorns on the ridges. Flowers perfect 68

67a Fruit black, sweet; leaves of new canes of three leaflets or sometimes simple; flowers often imperfect. Fig. 85.

WESTERN DEWBERRY
Rubus ursinus C. & S.

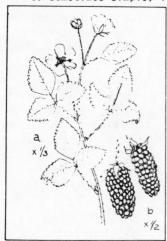

Figure 85

a, leaves and flower; b, fruit.

This is a native of our Pacific coast area. The flowers are about 1 inch across and white. The fruit when ripe is black, though white or red fruited plants sometimes occur. The canes stand erect at first but presently trail on the ground. Dewberries are usually a week or two earlier in ripening than blackberries. Where raised commercially they are usually supported on wires.

67b Fruit red, sour; leaves of new canes with 3 or 5 leaflets; flowers perfect. Fig. 86.

LOGANBERRY *Rubus loganobaccus* Bailey.

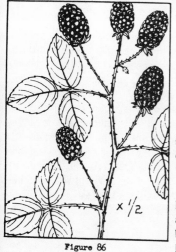

Figure 86

This berry which is also known as "Phenomenal" is raised extensively on our west coast. The flowers are white and showy, being 1½ to 2 inches across. The fruit is elongate and dark red.

The canes root at the tips. These young plants are set out in rows and the long flexible canes supported on wires. The crop is canned in large quantities for the market.

It has been often cited as a hybrid between the Red Raspberry and a blackberry but now seems to be a mutant variety of the Western Dewberry.

68a Leaflets on new canes usually narrow and small; canes often bristly as well as prickly. Fig. 87.

SOUTHERN DEWBERRY *Rubus trivialis* Michx.

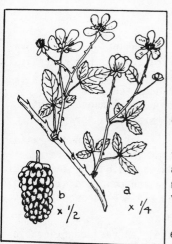

Figure 87

a, section of vine; b, mature fruit.

The stems of most dewberries are too flexible to stand unsupported and are trailing in habit. This one is native from Virginia through Florida to Texas. It has a tendency to be evergreen.

The leaves are 3 to 5 foliate; the flowers are about 1 inch across and white. It is the progenitor of several varieties valued by berry raisers.

Dewberries usually ripen earlier than blackberries. When raised commercially they are often supported on wire trellises or tied to stakes. The stems are biennials, the same as with the raspberries.

68b Leaflets on new canes large and broad; canes with small and weak prickles, scarcely hooked; no bristles; leaflet, broadest near base. **Fig. 88.**

EASTERN DEWBERRY <u>Rubus</u> <u>flagellaris</u> Willd.

Figure 88

a, part of vine; b, mature fruit.

This berry ranges throughout the East from Canada to the Gulf. Three leaflets are usual though five are sometimes seen. The flowers are supported on long pedicels; they are about 1 inch across and white. The calyx lobes are unusually large as are also the druplets composing the shining black fruit. The large, popular Lucretia dewberries are derived from this species.

69a Inflorescence long, without interspersed leaves and with gland tipped hairs. **Fig. 89.**

MOUNTAIN BLACKBERRY <u>Rubus</u> <u>allegheniensis</u> Porter.

Figure 89

a, stem and leaf; b, flower; c, fruit.

This is perhaps our best known wild and cultivated blackberry. It ranges from our eastern mountains to the Middle West and is the source of several named varieties commonly raised and marketed.

The canes of this species attain a height of 10 feet or more and are covered with vicious hooked prickles. The leaves are compound with 3 to 5 leaflets, and are pubescent on their lower surface.

Blackberries need considerable moisture and a fairly cool climate. They do not do well in the South if in dry regions. When this species grows in dry open patches it may be so short and small that it might not be recognized as this same species.

69b Inflorescence short and leafy; few if any glandular hairs; leaflets on fruiting stalks narrow, evenly toothed.
Fig. 90.   EARLY HARVEST BLACKBERRY **Rubus argutus** Link.

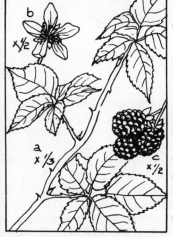

Figure 90

a, stem and leaves; b, flower; c, fruit.

This species may attain a height of five feet and has numerous prickles planted on the angles of the stem and on the petioles. Leaves with three and five leaflets. Fruit with but few seeds. There are other native species of blackberries and among the cultivated varieties, many named forms. Some are man-made species produced by hybridizing two different species to get a wholly new plant. Some of these are patented.

70a Fruit velvety (covered with pubescence); flowers and fruit sessile or practically so; flowers large, solitary, pink, appearing ahead of foliage. **71**

70b Fruit smooth (glabrous) **73**

71a Flowers pale pink, stone flattened, smooth except at margin; leaves broad, abruptly sharp pointed. Fig. 91.

COMMON APRICOT **Prunus armeniaca** L.

Figure 91

a, branch with leaves and fruit; b, flower.

This comes closest to the Peach of any of our fruits, and grows under somewhat similar conditions. The stone is much flattened and is not furrowed as with the peach. The flowers are ¾ to 1 inch across, pinkish to nearly white and appear very early. The fruit is yellow or reddish, somewhat flattened and breaks free from the stone. The Common Apricot originated in China, though it was long thought to have come from Armenia as the species name would indicate. The Black Apricot and the Japanese Apricot are used more as ornamentals than for their fruit. California produces more than 90% of our apricots.

71b Flowers darker, pink to reddish; stone furrowed and
pitted. **72**

72a Flesh of fruit soft and juicy when ripe; young leaves
sharply serrate; young twigs red on one side – green
on the other. Fig. 92.   **PEACH** Amygdalus persica **L.**

a, branch with leaves and fruit;
b, flowers; c, longitudinal section
of peach; d, "seed."

Again the species name would mis-
lead us. The peach, one of our most
valued fruit crops, originated in
China and not in Persia as sometimes
stated. The leaves are 5 to 9 inches
long and the bright pink flowers may
be up to 2 inches across. The fruit
which is from 1 to over 3 inches in
diameter is covered with fuzz.
There are several forms grown as
ornaments for their double flowers,
red foliage, etc. The NECTARINE
var. nucipersica is smooth skinned
and somewhat plum like. The FLAT
PEACH (sometimes "Saucer Peach")

Figure 92

var. platycarpa is very much flattened endwise.

72b Flesh hard, not eaten, splitting to the stone when mature,
stone a commercial "nut." Fig. 93.

ALMOND Amygdalus communis **L.**

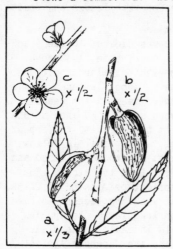

a, leaves; b, fruit; c, flowers.

This plant is peach-like but the
scarcely fleshy outer covering of
the fruit splits and is discarded
for it is the stone or "nut" which
is valued, the seed within being
eaten. The trees are 8 to 15 feet
high; the leaves 3-4 inches long,
the pink flowers up to 1½ inches
across and the fruit about 1½
inches long. This tree seems to
have originated in Western Asia.
Bitter Almonds are a variety of
this same tree. Prussic acid and
other extracts are made from the
bitter kernels. The "Flowering

Figure 93

Almond" grown for its Spring flowers is an entirely different
plant, though it belongs to this same genus.

73a Stone oval, flattened; smooth except for marginal pro-
     jection. PLUMS. 74
73b Stone globular, smooth. CHERRIES. 76
74a Leaves broad, reticulated, usually pubescent beneath;
     young twigs and fruit stems pubescent. Fig. 94.

COMMON or EUROPEAN PLUM Prunus domestica L.

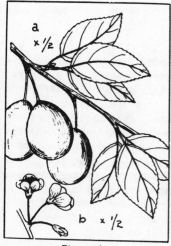

Figure 94

a, fruiting branch; b, flowers.

This tree has dull-green leaves
2-4 inches long, the flowers are
white or creamy, the fruit is
variable but usually bluish-purple,
and about 1½ inches long. Our
lowly prune is the dried fruit of
this tree. They are allowed to
fully ripen and drop from the
tree. They are then picked up,
sterilized in a lye solution and
dried. A variety insititia with
small shining dark green leaves
and deep blue fruit about an inch
or less in length is the common
Damson Plum.

74b Leaves relatively long, not reticulated, glabrous be-
     neath except on veins, finely serrate. Fig. 95.

JAPANESE PLUM Prunus salicina Lindl.

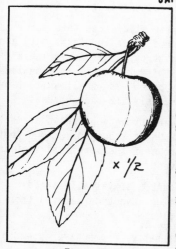

Figure 95

The twigs of these rather small
trees are smooth, shining and usually rather light colored. The
white flowers are from ½ to ¾ inch
across.

There are many named varieties
and the fruit varies widely in
size, shape and color. There are
no blue-purples however. The
plant originated in China. They
are quite hardy with us and seem
to thrive even better than our
native plums.

Brown-rot is likely the most
destructive of several plum
diseases. Among the insect
pests, the plum curculio is per-
haps most feared. The annual loss to plum growers from both
of these sources is heavy.

57

74c   Leaves coarsely serrate; young twigs usually smooth;
       fruit yellow or red (no blue-purples). Figs. 96-98.
       AMERICAN PLUMS. 7

75a   Trees to 20 or 30 feet, usually with thorns; flowers
       nearly 1 inch across; branches glabrous. Fig. 96.

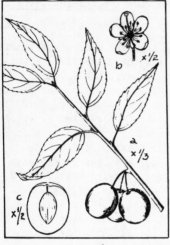

Figure 96

WILD PLUM Prunus americana Marsh.

a, fruit bearing branch; b, flower; c, section through plum.

This thorny tree reaches a height of 20 to 30 feet. It is a native of the eastern part of our country. The flowers are about 1 inch across. The fruit in the wild state is usually small and hard. Varieties have been selected and grown with plums more than 1 inch long and of excellent flavor. The fruit color is yellow or red, with yellow pulp. Many named varieties are known and sold by the nurseries. Other species of "wild" plums occur throughout our country.

75b   Much branched tree to 20 feet with zig-zag reddish branches
       flowers 1/3 inch across, white, before leaves. Fig. 97.

CHICKASAW PLUM Prunus angustifolia Mar.

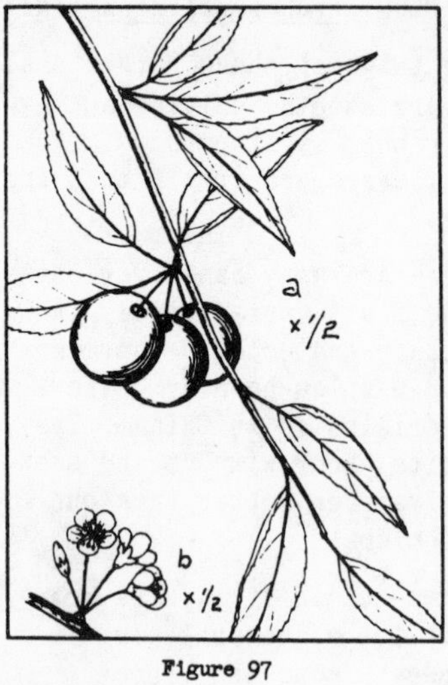

a, fruiting twig; b, flowers.

In its wild state this hardy tree bears red or yellow fruit only about $\frac{1}{2}$ inch through. It may reach a height of 20 feet but is sometimes only a bush. The small white flowers are only 1/3 inch across.

A variety watsoni known as the SAND PLUM is a bush of 3 to 6 feet and grows in the more arid West and Southwest.

A number of valuable named varieties have been derived from this plum.

Figure 97

Our native plums have extended the range of this valuable fruit into the warm, dry areas of the South and also farther north where the introduced species do not thrive.

58

75c Flowers ½ inch across, leaf petioles with two glands.
    Fig. 98.   WILD GOOSE PLUM Prunus hortulana Bailey.

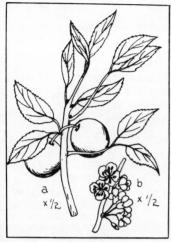

Figure 98

a, fruit bearing twig; b, flowers.

This is a small tree with thin bark and spreading branches. The leaves are 4-6 inches long and usually have two glands on the petiole. The flowers appear before the leaves and are about ½ inch across and white. The fruit is red with practically no bloom; flesh yellow. It is a native of the Middle West.

Here and there are other native plums that are gathered and eaten. Some of these have been cultivated and improved. It should not be understood that this at all concludes the list of edible plums.

76a Leaves comparatively long, point tapering, soft; fruit
    yellow or red, sweet. Fig. 99.
                                 SWEET CHERRY Prunus avium L.

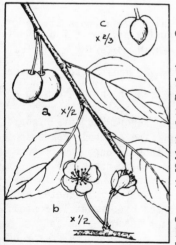

Figure 99

a, twig with fruit; b, flowers, c, cherry with stone.

This tree becomes large and tall with smooth peeling bark. The leaves are 4 to 10 inches long and flowers are white, about an inch across and hang rather limply. The fruit is solid with sweet flesh. In color it ranges from yellow to bright and dark red. Some varieties have heart shaped fruit.

Sweet Cherries grow successfully on the Pacific coast and in the East along the Great Lakes and the Hudson River. It is of European origin.

Brown-rot is a serious plant disease, and may result in heavy losses. Aphids and curculio are destructive insect pests.

76b Leaves short and wider than in 76a, abruptly pointed crisp; fruit bright or dark red, sour. Fig. 100.

SOUR CHERRY   Prunus cerasus L.

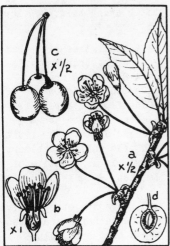

Figure 100

a, leaves and flowers; b, section of flower; c, cherries; d, fruit showing stone.

This is our common cultivated cherry which is widely distributed. The trees are broad topped, and comparatively small. The leaves are 3-4 inches long, stiff and shining. The flowers appear with the first leaves; they are white and about 1 inch across. The fruit is globular in outline, as is also its stone. Fruit colors are various shades of red.

While the per acre yield is not as large as that of Sweet Cherries this species has a much wider range and greater importance.

77a Core of fruit parchment-like or papery; each cell 1 to several seeded. 78

77b Core of fruit 5 bony carpels which are exposed at tip of fruit. Fruit solitary without a pedicel. Fig. 101.

MEDLAR   Mespilus germanica L.

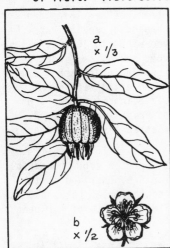

Figure 101

a, leaves and fruit; b, flower.

This tree or shrub grows to a height of 20 feet and is much raised in Europe and Asia Minor. The very fine toothed leaves are about 5 inches long, the flowers spread 1½ to 2 inches and are white or pinkish. The fruit may be over 2 inches in diameter and is hard and bitter until frosted, then after a "softening up" (bletting), they are eaten raw or cooked and the juice used as a beverage. Choice varieties are maintained by budding or grafting on pear, hawthorn or quince roots. The so-called "Japanese Medlar" is the Loquat (see Fig. 103).

78a Flowers in umbels appearing with the leaves. Fruit
glabrous. 79
78b Flowers and fruit solitary on ends of leafy stems; fruit
greenish yellow when ripe, firm, fuzzy. Fig. 102.

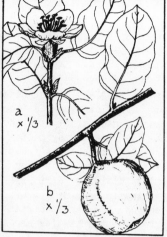

QUINCE Cydonia oblonga Mill.

a, flower and foliage; b, fruit.

This is the "true" quince. It originated in Asia and grows as a poorly formed tree or a shrub 10 to 20 feet high. The large flowers are white or tinged with pink, and have five styles and 20 stamens. The globular or pear-shaped fruit which is borne on the end of a twig may reach a diameter of 4 inches and is yellow or greenish yellow when ripe and highly fragrant. The fruit keeps poorly; it is used for butters and preserves and is so strongly flavored that a mixture of half or more of apples not only cheapen but improves the preserves.

Figure 102

The JAPANESE QUINCE with brilliant red flowers occasionally bears fruit. The CHINESE QUINCE (Chaenomeles sinensis) is planted in a limited way. Its fruit is large, often 6 or 7 inches long.

78c Flowers white, in terminal panicles. Evergreen shrub or
tree. Fig. 103.   LOQUAT Eribotrya japonica Lindl.

This evergreen shrub or tree attains a height of some 20 feet and has been introduced from China and Japan into our southern areas. The small branches are covered with rusty hairs; the flowers are white and spread ½ to ¾ inch. The down-covered fruit may be globular or pear-shaped, yellow or orange and up to 3 inches long. It is juicy when ripe but has many large seeds. It is eaten raw or made into jellies or preserves.

It is sometimes called the Japanese Medlar.

Figure 103

61

79a Flowers pink or rose, occasionally white; calyxtube open;
leaves dull; no stone cells in flesh. 80

79b Flowers white, calyxtube closed; leaves shining; fruit
usually "pear-shaped" flesh usually contains gritty stone
cells. Fig. 104.   PEAR Pyrus communis L.

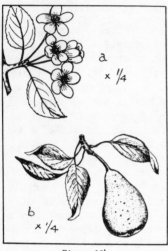

Figure 104

a, flowers and foliage; b, fruit

This tree of European origin, has
a long history and is grown rather
world wide. The trees become large
and old. The leaves are usually
smooth and shining and almost black
when dead. The flowers are an inch
or more across and faintly tinged
with pink. There are many cultivated varieties so that the fruit
ranges widely in size, shape and
flavor. The CHINESE or SAND PEAR
Pyrus serotina is sparingly grown
with us but has been crossed with
communis to give the Kieffer and
other hybrid varieties. The juice
drink made from pears is known as
perry.

80a Fruit retaining calyxlobes. Fig. 105.

APPLE Malus malus Britt

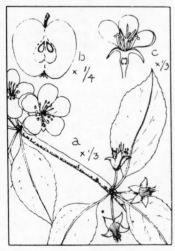

Figure 105

a, branch with flowers and young
fruit; b, section of apple, c, section through a flower.

This is one of our best known
fruits. It is represented by so
many varieties that the trees and
their fruit are quite variable.
The trees are comparatively low,
round topped, usually with oval
pubescent leaves. The ripe fruit
takes various shades of red, yellow, and green. The flowers are 1
to 2 inches across and tinged with
pink. Our present day choice
varieties are mutants which have
been selected from great numbers
of seedlings. They are propogated
and held true to type by budding or grafting. Trees raised
from their seeds yield "seedling" apples which are usually
somewhat similar to the wild parent, though an occasional one
might be highly superior.

80b Fruit when mature without calyx lobes; fruit yellow to red
     with waxy-like appearance. Fig. 106.

SIBERIAN CRAB *Malus baccata* Borkh.

a, fruiting branch; b, flower.

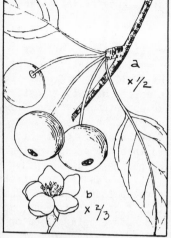

Figure 106

This is a fairly large wide-topped tree originally from East Asia. Its flowers are white and smaller than those of the apple. The fruit is red and yellow with a translucent waxy-appearing flesh, and often small (only a fraction of an inch in diameter). The PRAIRIE CRAB *Malus ioensis* Brit. produces a profusion of pink flowers that beautify our Mid-Western woods in springtime, and hard green "apples" with a pleasing wild flavor. In our Eastern states it gives place to the GARLAND CRAB *Malus coronaria* Mill. which closely resembles it.

SOULARDS CRAB has larger fruit. It is likely a hybrid.

81a Fruit a legume (pod opening at two opposite sides with the
     one-to-many seeds all attached at the same side. Usually
     with pea shaped flowers. Herbs, vines, shrubs or trees;
     leaves usually compound. Figs. 107-119. 82
81b Not as in 81a. 92
82a Herbaceous plants. 83
82b An evergreen tree to 50 feet high. Flowers red. Fig. 107.

CAROB *Ceratonia siliqua* L.

a, branch with fruit and leaves;
b, inflorescence; c, single flower.

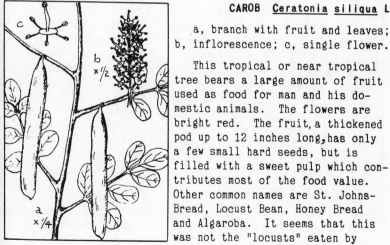

Figure 107

This tropical or near tropical tree bears a large amount of fruit used as food for man and his domestic animals. The flowers are bright red. The fruit, a thickened pod up to 12 inches long, has only a few small hard seeds, but is filled with a sweet pulp which contributes most of the food value. Other common names are St. Johns-Bread, Locust Bean, Honey Bread and Algaroba. It seems that this was not the "locusts" eaten by Saint John, for that was the grasshoppers of his region, a then much used food.

63

83a Leaflets lateral and even numbered, the leaf often term-
    inating in a tendril or bristle. 8x

83b Leaves with 3 leaflets one of which is terminal. 8C

84a Pod ripening under ground, wrinkled, constricted between
    seeds; flowers yellow. Fig. 108.

PEANUT Arachis hypogaea L.

Figure 108

The Peanut is native of Brazil
and is grown commercially in long
season, mild-climated regions. It
attains a height of 1 to 2 feet.
The rather conspicuous yellow flowers are sterile, but less showy
fertile flowers after pollination
are pushed into the ground by their
elongating pedicels where the nut
matures. It is unusual for a fruit
to thus develop under ground. The
nuts contain from 1 to 4 seeds, and
are roasted before being eaten or
made into Peanut Butter, oil or
Peanut Meal. Other names are
Ground Nut and Goober.

84b Pod ripening above ground. 8

85a Seeds spherical, (sometimes flattened by close contact
    in pod), often wrinkled when dry; flowers ½ to ¾ inch,
    white; sepals leaf-like. Fig. 109. PEA Pisum sativum L

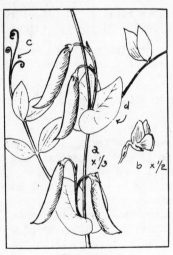

Figure 109

a, leaves and fruit; b, flower;
c, tendril; d, stipule.

Peas, like most of the cultivate
plants, are highly variable. Much
greater differences than would be
accounted necessary to make a new
species with wild plants, can be
given little attention in classifying cultigens to species. The
plant has pinnate leaves with the
terminal leaflet modified into a
tendril (c); a pair of stipules (d)
are often larger than the leaflets.
The normal form is climbing and may
reach a height of 6 feet; the
flowers are white and the pods flat
tened. A low bush form (var.
humile) is frequently raised in
gardens.

85b Seeds flattened, circular; sepals long, slender, pointed; flowers, small, whitish. Fig. 110.

LENTIL Lens esculenta Moench.

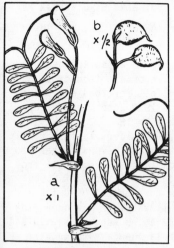

Figure 110

a, leaves and flowers; b, fruit.

This legume growing from 1 to 1½ feet high is much raised in Europe. Two rounded seeds are borne in each pod. These are used when fully ripe, in soups and stews. The plants are fed to domestic animals. The flowers are whitish and less than ½ inch long. The seeds are yellowish brown and lens shaped, hence the name. It will be noted that many plants used for food bear the species name "esculenta."

85c Seeds large, flattened and angled; flowers 1 to 1½ inches long, white with purple markings, sepals short and broad. Fig. 111.

BROAD BEAN Vicia faba L.

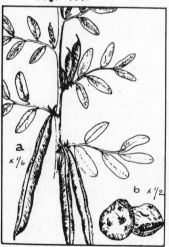

Figure 111

a, leaves and fruit; b, seeds.

This annual grows to a possible height of 6 feet. The flowers are more than an inch in length, whitish with a spot of purple. The fruit is long and heavy with the seed varying in size and shape but usually thick and often an inch across.

This is the "bean of history." Broad Beans do not thrive well in our climate so have never become popular in America.

Other names are Windsor and Horse Bean.

Beans have long been a favorite food of man. Early history reveals both the Egyptians and the Greeks prizing them. Native American species were used in a large way on both continents by the Indians before the coming of the white man.

86a Style bearded (hairy) near apical end. 87

65

86b Stems and leaves with many brown hairs. Style smooth near
     apical end. Bushy field annual 2-6 feet, much raised as a
     farm crop. Fig. 112.   SOYBEAN Glycine max Merr.

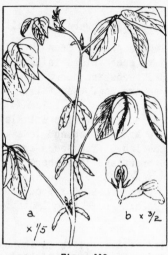

Figure 112

a, branch of plant; b, flower.

This plant has been introduced
from China and Japan and has become
a highly important farm crop, and a
source of oil for food and other
uses. In 1942 Henry County, Iowa,
which is only 18 by 24 miles in
size with considerable land not in
cultivation and several other crops
raised on large scale, still produced $1,500,000 worth of Soybeans.
It grows to a height of 2-5 feet,
with small white or lavender flowers. There are many varieties and
the globular seeds vary much in
color and markings. Soybeans are
frequently cut and threshed in the
field by using a combine.

87a Keel of corolla twisted spirally; leaves without tendrils.
     See Fig. 116b. 8

87b Keel curved but not twisted into a coil; pods long and
     slender. See Fig. 115c. 8

87c Keel bent inward at right angle, pods short and broad.
     Fig. 113.   HYACINTH BEAN Dolichos lablab L.

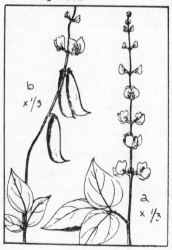

Figure 113

This bean is grown both for food
and as an ornamental. It is usually
a climber and may reach a length of
20-30 feet. The flowers vary from
white to deep purple and are nearly
an inch across; the pods are 2-3
inches long, flattened and often
purple. The seeds are white, purple
or black.

Other names are Bonavist and
Lablab. It probably originated in
the tropics where it is a perennial
but with us it is raised as an
annual. It is grown extensively
throughout the warmer parts of
Asia.

88a Slim hanging pods 1 to 2 feet long or longer. Fig. 114.

ASPARAGUS BEAN Vigna sesquipedalis Wight.

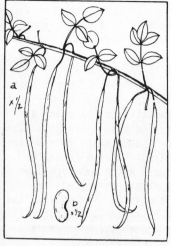

Figure 114

a, vine with pods; b, seed.

This, also known as the "Yard-Long Bean," is grown as a curiosity as well as for food. The pods are slender but sometimes actually reach a length of 3 feet or more. They are often much shriveled. The flowers are yellowish or violet, 2/3 to 1 inch long; the leaves attain a length of 5 inches. The seeds are about ½ inch long.

This bean likely originated in China and has long been cultivated in Europe.

88b Pods 6-12 inches long, hanging. Fig. 115.

COWPEA Vigna sinensis Endl.

Figure 115

a, leaves and fruit; b, seeds; c, flower.

This plant's principal use is for forage and soil improvement, but the seeds are often used for food. It is a vigorous grower and produces pods 8-12 inches long with heavy seeds ¼-½ inch long of several colors and variable markings.

It seems to have originated in Asia.

The YAM BEAN Pachyrhizus tuberosus is an important tropical food plant. Not only the young pods, but the tuberous roots are eaten.

The FLORIDA VELVET BEAN Stizolobium deeringianum is a white pubescent covered vine that attains a length of 50 feet and has some food value. LICORICE Glycyrrhiza glabra, much cultivated in Europe and Asia, is a bean-like plant.

89a Seeds flattened and broad, often about as wide as
long. 90

89b Seeds smaller, oblong or globular in shape. Calyx bracts
as large or larger than the calyx. Fig. 116.

KIDNEY BEAN Phaseolus vulgaris L.

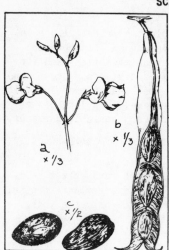

a, plant with fruit; b, flower.

This is our common garden bean,
and climbs by twining; the flowers
range from white to lavender and
are ½ inch or more in length. The
pods are 4 to 8 inches long and
may be either "string beans" or
"stringless" which refers to the
fibers that may or may not be in
the pod and which show up when the
pods are "snapped" for cooking.
Kentucky Wonder and other pole
varieties belong here.

Our common bush beans are var.
humilis, and they may be green or
yellow podded.

Figure 116

90a Flowers ½ inch or over, usually scarlet, though white in
one variety. Fig. 117.

SCARLET RUNNER Phaseolus coccineus L.

This one, known also as the
Multiflora Bean is often raised as
an ornamental. The flowers are
bright scarlet and nearly an inch
long. The pods are plump and 4 to
12 inches long, with seeds up to
an inch in length, black or dark
with red markings. It comes from
tropical America.

Var. albus is the WHITE DUTCH
RUNNER with white flowers and
seeds.

Bush forms of both of the
above are grown.

Figure 117

90b Flowers 1/8 to 3/8 inch long, whitish or cream colored. 91

91a Pods large with rolled edge; calyx bracts slim. Fig. 118.
LIMA BEAN *Phaseolus limensis* Macf.

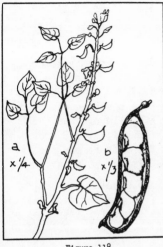

a, branch with flower and young fruit; b, pod with beans.

This tropical American bean is a perennial and in frost-free areas will continue to grow and produce for several years. In temperate regions it is raised as an annual. The pods are tough and woody so that only the shelled beans are eaten. These are marketed either green or dry. These seeds are often an inch broad and ½ inch thick. DWARF or BUSH LIMA is the variety *limenanus* which requires less care to raise. Beans are high in protein and have long been included in man's list of foods.

Figure 118

91b Pods long beaked with sharp edges; calyx bracts broadly rounded with prominent veins. Fig. 119.
SIEVA BEAN *Phaseolus lunatus* L.

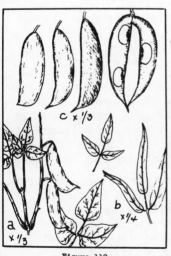

a, branch with fruit; b, types of leaves; c, types of pods.

This resembles the Lima Bean in shape of fruit and seeds. It too is likely of American origin. The leaflets are usually narrower than with the Limas. The greenish white flowers are small; the pods are 3-4 inches long by about an inch wide. The seeds are flat and thin and about ½ inch long. They are often white, but sometimes marked with red or brown in whole or part.

There are bush and narrow-leaved varieties.

Figure 119

93a Fruit with eight or more cells. 94
93b Fruit with but 3 to 5 cells. Fig. 120.
                  OVAL KUMQUAT Fortunella margarita Swingle.

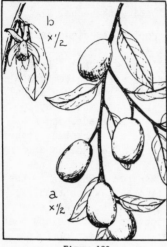

a, leaves and fruit; b, flower.

Kumquats are the dwarfs of the citrus group, these shrubs or small trees only reaching a height of 10 to 12 feet. The fruit of Nagami, here pictured, is oblong and only a little over an inch long with leaves 1½ to 3 inches in length. The flowers are fleshy, white and with 20 stamens.

Two other species, both with globular fruit, are grown. MEIWA Fortunella crassifolia Sw. has an almost juiceless pulp while MARUMI Fortunella japonica Sw. has acid juice and is more prized for eating

Figure 120·

These plants are often raised as dwarf pot-plants. The fruit is eaten – frequently, rind and all – and used in salads.

94a Petioles winged or margined, blades of leave attached to petiole in usual way. 95
94b Leaves apparently un-attached to tip of petiole, petiole without wings; fruit with thick rind which is candied.
     Fig. 121.   CITRON Citrus medica L.

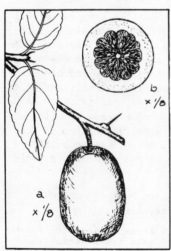

a, fruit and leaves; b, cross section of fruit.

The leaves of this shrub or tree grow from 4 to 8 inches long. The pale yellow oblong fruit reaches a length of 7 inches. The flowers are white with lilac exteriors and have about 30 stamens.

The pulp and juice is similar to the lemon but less acid. The spongy rind is the part most largely used. It is candied and used in fruit cakes, preserves, etc. It is grown, most largely, in the Mediterranean region.

Etrog, used in Jewish ceremonies, is the wild form of the Citron.

Figure 121

95a Leaf petioles winged, flower buds white. **96**
95b Leaf petioles margined but not winged; flower buds tinted
     with pink on outside; fruit very sour. Fig. 122.

LEMON Citrus limonia Osbeck.

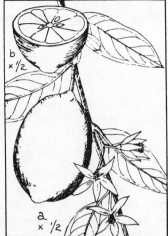

a, branch with flowers and fruit;
b, cross section of a lemon.

California produces most of the
lemons on our markets. It is a
small thorny tree with leaves 2½ to
4 inches long. The flowers are
white with pinkish exterior.
Lemons are picked green when they
will no longer go through a ring
2⅛ inches in diameter. They are
put in cold storage and treated, to
give them color as they are needed.
Several varieties are raised. In
one the fruit may attain a length
of almost 10 inches.

Figure 122

96a Flowers more than I inch across; fruit spherical or flat-
     tened at poles, mildly sour or sweet. **97**
96b Flowers less than I inch across, fruit elongated at
     poles, I to 2 inches in diameter, juice very sour.
     Fig. 123.   **LIME Citrus aurantifolia Swingle.**

a, branch with leaves and thorns;
b, cross section of fruit.

These thickly branched trees
bear leaves 2-3 inches long. The
flowers are white and about ½ inch
across. The fruit is smaller than
that of the lemon which it resembles. The juice is highly acid.
It is used in much the same way as
the lemon. Most of those on the
market come from south of the
United States. The tree and fruit
are very easily damaged by frost.
Fresh limes are highly perishable.
The LIMEQUAT has been produced by
crossing the Lime with the Oval
Kumquat. It produces a pale yellow fruit a little less than 3
inches long.

Figure 123

71

97a Fruit less than 4 inches in diameter, deep yellow to vermilion when ripe; twigs glabrous. **98**

97b Fruit usually 4 inches or more in diameter, pale yellow; twigs pubescent. Fig. 124.

GRAPEFRUIT Citrus paradisi Sw.

Figure 124

a, branch with fruit; b, cross section of fruit.

The Spaniards introduced this plant into Florida in the 16th century. It is a large, round-topped glossy-leaved tree which bears its fruit in axillary clusters from which it has derived its name. The leaves are 3 to 6 inches long, with a characteristic broad-winged petiole. The white flowers are about one inch across, while the pale yellow fruit has a diameter of 4 to 6 inches. The flesh is normally pale yellow, though there are pink fleshed varieties, and seedless forms.

The SHADDOCK or PUMMELO (Citrus maxima Merr.) is much like the Grapefruit. Its fruit is large, weighing as much as seven pounds each.

98a Leaf petioles with narrow wings. **99**

98b Leaf petioles with very broad wings; fruit acid.
Fig. 125.   SEVILLE ORANGE Citrus aurantium L.

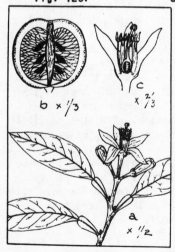

Figure 125

a, branch with leaves and flowers; b, longitudinal section through fruit; c, flower section.

This "Sour Orange" is grown in Southern Europe for use in beverages and preserves. Perfumery is made from the flowers. It is a medium-sized, much-spined tree with leaves some 4 inches in length, very fragrant white flowers, and globular fruit about 3 inches in diameter. This species is hardier than other citrus plants and is much used as stock on which other species are grafted. The TRIFOLIATE ORANGE Poncirus trifoliata is a hardy ornamental with small orange-like fruit.

99a Outer covering of fruit tight; juice sweet. Fig. 126

ORANGE <u>Citrus sinensis</u> Osbeck.

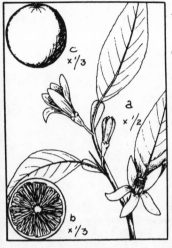

Figure 126

a, flowers and foliage; b, section through fruit; c, fruit.

This "Sweet Orange" seems to have originated in Southeast Asia. The trees are medium sized, with flowers white and very fragrant. It is now grown at many favorable places along our southern border from Florida to California.

It is desirable to supply the market throughout the entire twelve months. To do this, different varieties of oranges are raised. In California the Navel Orange from Brazil is on the market from November till April when the Valencias (from Spain) begin to ripen and are marketable until November.

Other orange raising regions cover the seasons with varieties suited to their growing conditions.

99b Fruit sweet; outer covering loose when ripe; segments usually exceeding 10. Fig. 127.

SATSUMA ORANGE <u>Citrus nobilis</u> var. <u>unshiu</u> Swingle.

Figure 127

a, foliage; b, fruit.

<u>Citrus nobilis</u> is a thornless species with small white flowers and much flattened fruit with rough loose skin of a vermilion shade. Its juice is very sweet.

The Satsumas (var. <u>unshiu</u>) are a hardy variety with delightful flavor.

The TANGERINE and MANDARIN ORANGES (var. <u>delicosa</u>) have similar but smaller fruit than the Satsuma.

The CALAMONDIN ORANGE <u>Citrus mitis</u> Blanco, a native of the Philippines bears small fruit (about 1 inch across) with loose skin. It is occasionally seen in our country.

100a Herbs with small flowers borne in
      umbels (a) (usually compound).
      Fruit dry, splitting into 2 seeds
      (b). Fig. 128. 101

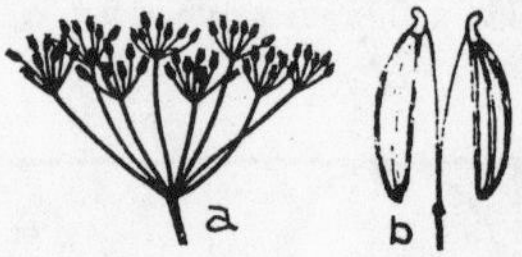

Figure 128. a, compound umbel; b, seeds separated from one fruit.

100b Plants not as in 62a. 112

101a Fleshy underground parts used for food. 102

101b Leaves eaten. 104

101c Fruit ("seeds") used for seasoning. 106

102a Fleshy taproot eaten. 103

102b Tuberous roots eaten. Leaves once-pinnately compound,
      flowers white. Fig. 129.   SKIRRET Sium sisarum L.

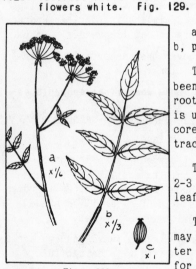

a, branch with leaves and fruit; b, pinnately compound leaf; c, fruit

This Eastern Asiatic plant has been used in Europe for its edible roots much as the vegetable oyster is used. The roots have a woody core which must be removed and detracts from its popularity.

The plant reaches a height of 2-3 feet. The leaves have 3 to 7 leaflets. The flowers are white.

The clustered tuber-like roots may be left in the ground over winter or dug in the fall and stored for winter use.

Figure 129

This Parsley or Carrot Family (Umbelliferae) is a highly important one. Its some 2000 plants are scattered the world over and make valuable contributions to food, flavoring and medicine. Some of its species such as the Poison-Hemlock contain rank poisons. The hollow ridged stems and deeply furrowed seeds together with their pungent odor, are characteristic of most of the species.

103a Roots yellow to deep orange, flowers white, leaves finely cut. Fig. 130.

CULTIVATED CARROT Daucus carota var. sativa DC.

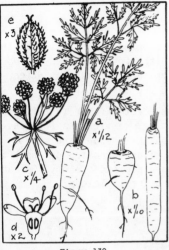

Figure 130

a, plant with edible root; b, other forms of roots; c, compound umbel with flowers; d, flower section; e, fruit.

Don't neglect your carrots if your eyes need help. Our population was once divided into two groups, those who liked carrots and those who did not. Now we all eat them, regardless.

Var. sativa is usually a biennial and has a thick taproot that runs to several shapes with the different varieties. The deep yellow to salmon-red color is evidence of the carotin it contains. Var. carota is the wild or escaped carrot sometimes known as Queen Anne's Lace, the name referring to its flat topped finely divided inflorescence of tiny white flowers. Its root is slim and rather woody.

103b Roots tapering, white; flowers greenish-yellow, leaves pinnately compound, with coarse leaflets. Fig. 131.

CULTIVATED PARSNIP Pastinaca sativa L.

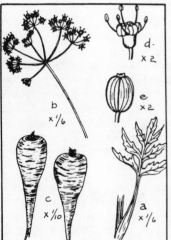

Figure 131

a, leaf; b, compound umbel of flowers; c, typical roots; d, single flower; e, fruit.

Like the Carrot, the Parsnip has both a wild and cultivated variety. The escape form with slender inedible root is widely naturalized in waste land. It is var. sylvestris.

This perennial reaches a height of 5 feet the second year when it produces its greenish-yellow flowers and seeds. The grooved stems are coarse and hollow. The fleshy taproots may live out of doors through the winter and seem to be the better for being frozen. The root flesh is a dull white.

Parsnips have been cultivated since the days of early Rome.

103c Root globular with several thick branches below, white inside; flowers white; leaves pinnately compound. Fig. 132.
CELERIAC Apium graveolens var. rapaceum DC.

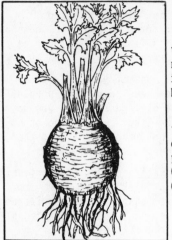

Figure 132

This is only a less known form of the common Celery. In this case the reserve plant food has been stored in a thick turnip-like root which has about the same flavor as celery.

It has greater favor in Europe than with us. It is used for flavoring, cooked in soups and stews, put into salads or eaten by itself. Other names are Knob Celery, German Celery and Turnip Celery.

104a Entire leaf used for seasoning or garnishing. 1

104b Thickened petiole eaten raw or cooked. Fig. 133.
CELERY Apium graveolens var. dulce DC

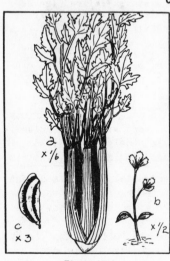

Figure 133

a, typical bunch of celery; b, seedling; c, celery seed.

There is a short thick stem (heart) which supports the roots below and from which the fleshy-petioled leaves arise. The plant is marketed at the end of the first season. During the second year flowers and seeds are produced. The flowers are white and borne in compounds umbels. Celery seed is ground to make celery salt or used ground or whole in pickels and relishes.

Various schemes of "blanching" the stalks are used, such as putting boards on each side of the row or banking with earth. The threads so apparent in the stalks (leaf petioles) are the vascular bundles of the transporting system.

105a Leaflets divided into 3 parts, flowers greenish-yellow.
Fig. 134.   PARSLEY Petroselinum hortense Hoffm.

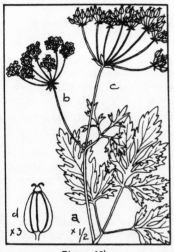

a, branch with leaf; inflorescence of flowers (b) and of seeds (c); d, fruit.

The leaves of this low-growing plant are used for garnishing and for seasoning. It seems to have originally come from Egypt but has been much raised in Europe and America. The flowering and fruiting stalks may attain a height of 2 feet. The flowers are greenish.

The common parsley has leaves as here pictured but var. crispum with much curled leaves is a strong favorite.

TURNIP-ROOTED or HAMBURG PARSLEY var. radiocosum has thick white roots

Figure 134

2 inches by 6 or 8 inches long, resembling parsnips and is used in much the same way.

105b Leaflets not in 3's, finely cut; flowers white. Fig. 135.
SALAD CHERVIL Anthriscus cerefolium Hoffm.

a, branch with leaf and fruit; b, flower; c, fruit; d, cross section of seed.

This is a somewhat hairy annual that grows to a height of about 2 feet. The flowers are white and the fruit elongated and black. The leaves resemble parsley. It is used in salads and soups. There is a curled leaf variety.

TURNIP-ROOTED CHERVIL, Chaerophyllum bulbosum L. is raised for its 2-4 inch long underground tubers.

Figure 135

105c Leaflets not in 3's, finely cut; flowers yellow. DILL. 108a.

106a Fruit not bristly; plants 1 to 3 feet high or higher. . 10?
106b Fruit bristly; plants only about 6 inches high; flowers
     white or rose. Fig. 136.   CUMIN Cuminum cyminum L.

a, entire plant; b, branch of fruiting head.

This little herb gets up to only six inches. The leaves are finely cut and the flowers white or rose-tinted. The small seeds are used for spicing or flavoring many food products such as soups, salads, bread, cheese and pickles.

It has been long known in Europe and Asia. Several herbs of this family are mentioned in the Bible, this being one of them.

Figure 136

107a Fruit nearly spherical; outer flowers of each secondary
     umbel with petals ray-like. Fig. 137.

CORIANDER Coriandrum sativum L.

a, leaf; b, compound umbel of fruit; c, single fruit.

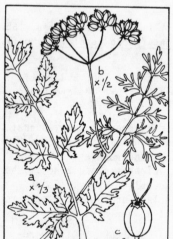

This is a strong-smelling plant, growing to a height of 1 to 3 feet. The flowers are white and the fruit nearly spherical. These fruit "seeds" are used in seasoning and are sometimes coated with colored sugar icing and used for decorating cakes, etc.

The members of this family are alike in having oil-carrying tubes running the length of the stem. It is these volatil oils which give the characteristic odors and flavors to the plants. There is no question about the potency of some of these oils, but opinions differ widely as to which ones are liked for food flavorings.

Figure 137

107b Not as in 107a. 108

108a Leaves very finely cut so that ultimate divisions are
      linear; fruit flattened. Fig. 138.

                              DILL Anethum graveolens L.

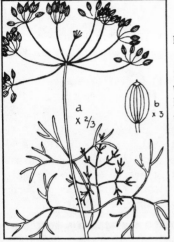

Figure 138

a, branch with leaves and compound umbel of fruit; b, fruit.

This plant is best known through its contribution to the pickles which bears its name. It reaches a height of 2 to 3 feet with smooth stems and finely-divided leaves. The flowers are yellowish-green. The slightly winged seeds are employed in flavoring sauces and pickles.

Some prefer to use the leaves instead of the seeds as they have seemingly a better flavor.

108b Outer segments of leaves broader fruit not flattened. 109

109a Leaf segments in 3's. 110

109b Most of the leaf segment not in 3's; Fruit elongated
      curved, flowers white. Fig. 139. CARAWAY Carum carvi L.

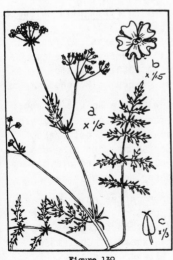

Figure 139

a, leaves, flowers, fruit; b, flower in detail; c, single fruit.

This plant is usually about 2 feet high. The flowers are white and the seeds elongated.

The seeds are put into bread and cheese, as well as being used for candy and perfume making. The plant has a fleshy taproot not unlike the parsnip. This root is eaten as a vegetable. The roots and young shoots are sometimes used in stews.

The plant is a native of Germany and Holland but sometimes grows spontaneously with us.

110a Leaf petioles thickened; flowers white. Seed ground
      into "celery salt." Fig. 133. CELERY. 104b

110b Flowers yellowish; petioles not thickened 111

111a Flowers greenish-yellow; stems heavy. Fig. 140.
                        LOVAGE Levisticum officinale Koch.

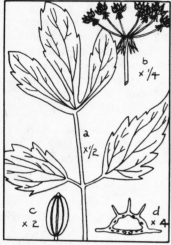

a, leaf; b, inflorescence of
fruit; c, fruit; d, cross section of
seed.

Lovage is a native of Italy. The
stems, leaves, and tender shoots are
sometimes used in salad and stews
but it is the seed which is princi-
pally employed for food as in candy
making or other seasoning.

The plant may attain a height of
6 feet and has coarsely-toothed,
three-parted leaves. The flowers
are greenish-yellow or sometimes
pinkish. Other names are Italian
Lovage and Garden Lovage.

Figure 140

111b Flowers yellowish-white, annual. Fig. 141.
                        ANISE Pimpinella anisum L.

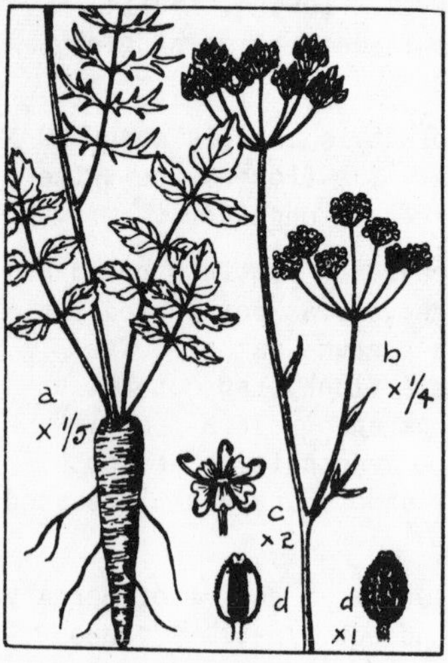

a, root and leaves; b, fruiting
branch with flowers and seeds;
c, flower in detail; d, side and
edge views of fruit (2 seeds).

The plant has a height of about
2 feet. The flowers are yellowish-
white and small. It belongs to
the Mediterranean countries and
Germany. The seeds and oil are
used in candy and cookie making.

The German anise cakes are an
essential part of the Christmas
season in many homes. They are
baked weeks ahead of Christmas
time and allowed to age.

Figure 141

112a Petals united into a tubular
corolla, usually with two lips
(a); plant stems usually square
in cross section (b); plants
characterized by their volatile
oil. Fig. 142. MINT FAMILY. . 113

Figure 142. a, typical
mint flowers; b, cross
section of stem.

112b Plants not as in 112a 119

113a Flowers with four perfect stamens 114

113b With but two perfect stamens; leaves and stems white,
woolly. Flowers blue, purple or white. Fig. 143.

SAGE Salvia officinalis L.

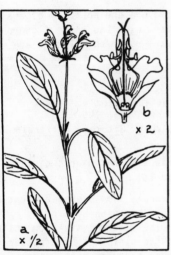

Figure 143

a, branch with leaves and flowers; b, section of flower showing
parts.

This semi-shrubby perennial, 6
to 15 inches high, is grown in
many gardens, for its leaves and
stems make a favorite seasoning
for sausages, dressings, etc. The
leaves are usually gray with a
whitish woolly growth. The flowers range from white to violet or
blue. It is a native of the
Mediterranean region.

It is used either fresh or dried.

SCARLET SAGE or "SALVIA" Salvia
splendens, a Brazilian shrub growing to a height of 8 feet, is a
very popular ornamental with us, where it is seen in yards and
parks covered with a profusion of scarlet flowers. The first
frost kills it, so it is grown here as an annual.

Dozens of other species of Sage are known for their attractive flowers. TEXAS SAGE Salvia coccinea, and MEXICAN RED
SAGE Salvia fulgens both have large bright red flowers somewhat like the foregoing.

114a Floral bracts (leaves at base of flowers and fruit)
about as large as the stem leaves. 115

114b Floral bracts much smaller than the stem leaves. . . 116

81

115a Stamens longer than the corolla; leaves about 1/3 as wide
      as long. Fig. 144.   HYSSOP Hyssopus officinalis L.

Figure 144

a, branch with flowers and leaves
b, leaves.

This little herb, growing about 10
to 20 inches high, finds use as a
pot-herb and for flavoring. The
leaves and young stems are used in
salads and the flowers employed to
flavor soup. "Hyssop tea" is made
from the dried flowering branches.
For this purpose they are picked
while still in the bud stage.

The flowers are normally blue although var. alba has white flowers
and in var. ruber the flowers are
red.

115b Stamens about the same length as the corolla; leaves
      linear, about 1/6 as wide as long. Fig. 145.
                        SUMMER SAVORY Satureja hortensis L.

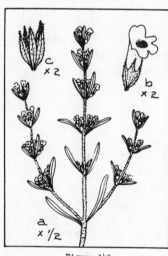

Figure 145

a, branch with flowers; b, flower; c, fruit.

This annual herb averages about a
foot in height, with soft hairy
leaves. The flowers vary from white
to bluish to pink. It is a rather
common escape having been introduced from Europe.

The leaves are used fresh, or
dried for flavoring soups and dressings much the same as sage.

WINTER SAVORY Satureja montana L.
also known as Mountain Savory is a
perennial which is similarly used.

CALAMINT Satureja calamintha
and ALPINE SAVORY Satureja alpina are related herbs which are
grown and used in Europe for seasoning. Both are low, somewhat
creeping plants. Other species are sometimes grown as border
ornamentals.

116a Leaves more than ½ inch wide. 117
116b Leaves less than ¼ inch wide; plant less than 1 foot
      high; flowers in open terminal clusters; calyx 2 lipped.
      Fig. 146.   THYME Thymus vulgaris L.

a, branch of plant; b, flower.

This little shrub attains a height of only 6 or 8 inches and is covered with a whitish pubescence. The flowers are lilac colored. It is used for seasoning much like sage. For drying, the upper branches are picked when blossoming begins.

MOTHER-OF-THYME Thymus serphyllum has similar uses. It is prostrate in habit and is also called Creeping Thyme. Several varieties have been developed differing in the colors of flowers and leaves. Both of these plants are natives of Southern Europe.

Figure 146

117a Teeth on leaves sharp pointed. 118
117b Teeth on leaves rounded at tips. Fig. 147 . . .
                              CATNIP Nepeta cataria L.

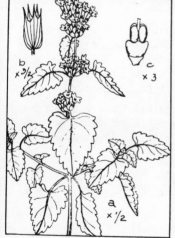

a, flowering branch; b, fruit; c, four-parted ovary characteristic of the mints.

This old-world plant is now widely scattered in America. It attains a height of some 3 feet, is soft with short pubescence and has pale lavendar flowers.

It is sometimes used for seasoning and for making "catnip tea." Its quality is best when first blooming. Cats are particularly fond of it. Other names are Catmint and Catnep.

Several species of this genus are cultivated mostly as bedding plants. GROUND IVY or Nepeta hederacea is the best known. It is a creeping plant with rounded leaves and is very hardy.

Figure 147

118a Leaves sessile; spikes slim, scattered. Fig. 148.
                                SPEARMINT Mentha spicata L.

Figure 148

a, branch with leaves and flowers; b, single flower.

This glabrous, herbaceous perennial grows to a height of a foot or
more and is a bright green with
clear white flowers. It is a native
of Europe but is widely naturalized
in our country. Its chief use is in
chewing gum though it also finds use
as seasoning and for making a beverage.

PENNYROYAL Mentha pulegium L. is
preferred by some to spearmint.

118b Leaves with short petioles; spikes thick and compact.
      Fig. 149.   PEPPERMINT Mentha piperita L.

Figure 149

a, flowering shoot; b , flower;
c, fruit.

The mints spread by means of
their rootstalks. Peppermint may
reach a height of 3 feet. The flowers are lavender or purple, - rarely
white. It is of European origin.

When raised commercially, the
plants are cut and dried as with
hay. The oil is then extracted by
use of steam.

Several other mints of this same
genius find occasional food uses.

119a Herbs (rarely shrubs) with star-shaped flowers and 2-5
      celled, many seeded, fleshy berry (sometimes a dry
      capsule). Figs. 150-160. NIGHTSHADE FAMILY. 120

119b Plants not as in 119a 130

120a Common succulent garden or field plant, bearing underground starchy tubers. Fig. 150.

POTATO Solanum tuberosum L.

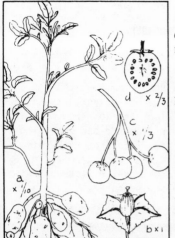

Figure 150

a, plant with tubers; b, flower;
c, fruit (seed balls); d, longitudinal section of fruit showing seeds.

This highly important food plant
is a native of South America.   The
plant is grown by planting pieces of
the tubers raised the preceding
year.   The plant reaches a height
of 1 to 3 feet and some varieties
produce abundant white or lavender
flowers and fruit balls.   The fruit
resembles small green tomatoes.   The
seed thus produced may be planted.
The first year their tubers are
small, but these small tubers will
grow plants that produce normal
sized potatoes.   New varieties are
secured this way, but these seedlings are usually inferior to
their parents.   Tomato scions have been grafted on potato plants
so that while potato tubers are produced underground, tomato
fruit ripen on the same plant.   This makes an interesting
novelty, but has scant practical value.

120b Not bearing underground tubers. 121
121a Fruit fleshy. 122
121b Fruit dry with very fine seeds; leaves long and broad,
used for smoking, chewing and snuff. Fig. 151.

TOBACCO Nicotiana tabacum L.

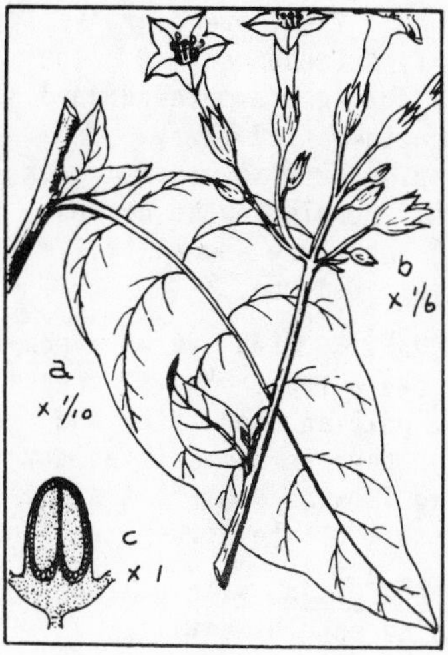

a, typical leaf; b, flowers;
c, fruit showing seeds.

This annual plant growing to a
height of several feet and producing long, broad leaves is a native
of South America.   The flowers are
from 1½ to 2 inches long and pale
pink to rose.   The fruit is a dry
capsule which contains many very
small seeds.   There are numerous
varieties raised commercially.

122a Fruit not enveloped within
an enlarged calyx. . . . 123
122b Fruit greenish, yellow or
purple berry, enclosed in
a greatly enlarged sac
like calyx. 128

Figure 151

123a Fruit bluish-black or purplish when ripe. 124
123b Fruit red or yellow when ripe 125
124a Fruit ½ inch or less in diameter; flowers small, white with yellow center, plants glabrous. Fig. 152.

Figure 152

WONDERBERRY Solanum nigrum L.

a, branch with leaves and fruit; b, berry; c, flower.

This rather common weed has been improved (?) by selection until the bluish-black berries grow to nearly ½ inch in diameter and are eaten raw or made into preserves, etc. The plant may reach a height of 3 feet. It has white flowers and is an abundant producer.

Other names are Garden Huckleberry, Morelle and Sunberry.

124b Fruit up to several inches in diameter; leaves large irregular; gray, tomentose. Fig. 153.

COMMON EGGPLANT Solanum melongena var. esculentum Nees.

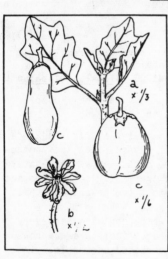

Figure 153

a, branch with leaves; b, flower; c, fruit.

This sturdy growing plant is usually covered with a long gray pubescence. The flowers are violet and nearly 2 inches across. The fruit is a large, smooth-skinned, rather solid-meated berry. The fruit varies much in shape, color and size. Purple is the common color though there are white, yellow and striped ones.

The SNAKE EGGPLANT var. serpentinum grows a fruit some 12 inches long but only an inch thick and curled. There is a dwarf variety producing flowers and fruit smaller than that of the Common Eggplant.

The SCARLET EGGPLANT Solanum integrifolium, with scarlet or yellow fruit 2 inches across, is used as an ornamental.

125a Anthers closely surrounding the style. Fruit
smooth. **126**

125b Stamens and anthers spreading; fruit wrinkled or
somewhat irregular. **127**

126a Tropical, tree-like, soft, hairy, woody shrub to 10
feet high. Leaves simple, cordate to a foot long.
Fruit egg shaped, 3 inches long, dark red. Fig. 154.

TREE-TOMATO Cyphomandra betacea Sen.

a, leaf; b, fruit.

This somewhat woody shrub grows
to a height of 6 to 10 feet. The
fragrant flowers are ½ inch across
and pink. The egg shaped fruit is
about 3 inches long. It is dark
red or brownish and resembles the
common tomato in flavor.

It is a tropical plant and can
be grown only in greenhouses in
temperate regions.

Figure 154

126b Leaves pinnately compound, hairy, strong smelling; flowers
yellow. Fig. 155.

TOMATO Lycopersicon esculentum var. commune Bailey.

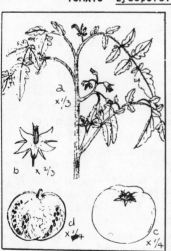

a, branch with leaves and flowers; b, flower; c, typical fruit;
d, longitudinal section through
fruit.

The young plants stand erect
but topple over as they grow larger and begin to develop fruit.
The vine may become 6 feet or more
in length. The flowers are yellow, and the fruit yellow, scarlet
or "purple" red.

Not so many years ago tomatoes
were thought to be poisonous and
were grown only for ornament and
called "Loveapples." Their importance as a food has increased
rapidly largely on account of

Figure 155

their favorable vitamin contents.

127a Fruit large puffy, depressed at base, variously shaped;
       mild flavor. Yellow or red when ripe. Fig. 156.

SWEET or BELL PEPPERS Capsicum frutescens
var. grossum Bailey.

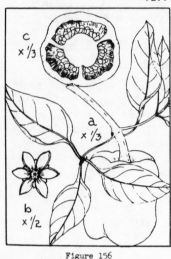

Figure 156

a, branch with leaves and fruit;
b, flower (5 petals are normal but
cultigens often have extras);
c, cross section of fruit showing
many seeds.

This plant is really a tropical
shrub but is grown with us as an
annual, since the early frosts kill
it. In frost-free areas it may
reach a height of 8 feet, but in
our one season, 2 to 3 feet is a
good height. The leaves are
glabrous and 1 to 5 inches long;
the flowers are white or greenish-
white. Fruit colors when ripe are
yellow, red and dark violet. The
Sweet Pepper is mild flavored and
used in salads and relishes or "stuffed" and pickled.

127b Fruit smaller than 127a, of various shapes; flavor usually
       fiery (a very little goes a long-long ways.) Fig. 157.

RED PEPPERS Capsicum frutescens L.

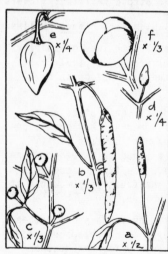

Figure 157

Under this heading it is chosen
to include several groups of the
species other than the Sweet Peppers. In this we follow Erwin.

TABASCO GROUP (a); erect,
elongate, very "hot" fruit with
cup-like calyx; flowers small.
CAYENNE GROUP (b); called chili or
finger peppers have long curved
pods 4 to 12 inches in length.
The calyx is cup-shaped. CHERRY
GROUP (c); small globular fruit on
long erect pedicels, orange or red.
This and the groups that follow
have saucer-shaped calyx cups.
CELESTIAL GROUP (d); fruit ¾ to 1¼
inches long, erect first yellow-
green then light purple and finally orange red. PERFECTION
GROUP (e); pods 3 to 4 inches long, hanging, bright red.
TOMATO GROUP (f); fruit 2-4 inches in diameter, usually with 4
cells, yellow or red. These are sometimes called Pimentos.

128a Stems pubescent or hairy; berry yellow when ripe. . . 129
128b Stems glabrous; berry purplish. Fig. 158.

TOMATILLO Physalis ixocarpa Brot.

a, branch with fruit in husks; b, flower; c, section through husk showing berry.

This glabrous annual grows to a height of 3 to 4 feet. The bright yellow flowers are ½ inch across and have 5 brown spots in the throat. The inflated calyx as it surrounds the berry is purple veined. The berry is sticky, purple and many seeded. It has been introduced from Mexico.

If ground cherries when picked are left in the husk they will keep through the winter.

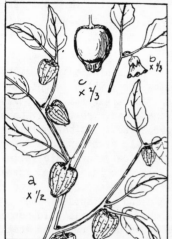

Figure 158

129a Plants to I foot high, often prostrate, anthers yellow. Berry sticky when ripe. Fig. 159.

STRAWBERRY-TOMATO Physalis pubescens L.

a, branch with flowers and fruit; b, fruit in calyx and husk.

This plant is rather prostrate and reaches a height of about a foot. The leaves are soft, and both they and the stems are pubescent. The flowers are less than ½ inch long and pale yellow with 5 brown spots in the throat. The anthers are yellow.

The calyx, rather short at flowering times, elongates to completely enclose the yellow fruit which becomes about ½ inch in diameter.

This is the most common garden ground cherry. The berries are eaten raw or cooked in several ways, and are sometimes used in

Figure 159

pickles. The plant is native throughout much of our country and also in tropical America.

129b Plants to 3 feet high; anthers blue or purple; fruit not sticky when ripe. Fig. 160.

CAPE-GOOSEBERRY *Physalis peruviana* L.

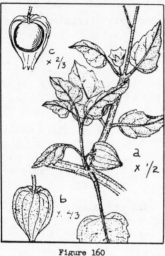

Figure 160

a, branch with flower and fruit; b, fruit in husk; c, husk split to show berry.

This species also bears a globular yellow berry which is not sticky. The plant is larger than the Strawberry-Tomato and more thickly covered with pubescence. Its berry is less sweet. It may stand up to 3 feet high. The flowers are pale yellow and usually more than ½ inch across. There are purple spots and veins in the petals and the anthers are bluish-purple. Several wild members of this genus could be eaten much the same as the three described here. The CHINESE LANTERN Plant is very showy with large bright red calyx "pods."

130a Herbaceous vines with lateral tendrils; fruit fleshy, (a pepo) with a rind and spongy seed.bearing center. CUCURBITACEAE. 131
130b Plants not as in 130a. 138
131a Edible fruits with many seeds. 132
131b Large edible fruit with but one large seed. Fig. 161.

CHAYOTE *Sechium edule* Sw.

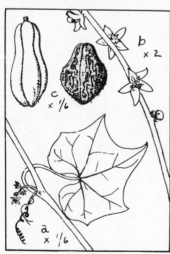

Figure 161

a, section of vine showing leaf, tendril and staminate flowers; b, staminate flowers; c, fruit.

This large tender vine grows from perennial tubers. The flowers are small and whitish. The fruit is usually pale green, 3 to 8 inches long and resembles a squash. It has but one seed, a flattened disk-like structure 1 to 2 inches across. The fruit, of which there may be 100 borne on one vine are used much the same as summer squashes. The entire fruit is planted or new plants are raised from cuttings. It is popular in our southernmost states. Other names are Mango Squash, Merliton and Christophine.

90

132a Petals distinctly united into a large yellow bell-
      shaped flower. 133

132b Petals distinct, or if united the corolla lobes cut
      and separated for more than half their length. 134

133a Leaves prickly, deeply cut between the lobes; fruit
      stalk angular, expanding at point of attachment. Fig. 162.
         FIELD AND OTHER PUMPKINS Cucurbita pepo L.

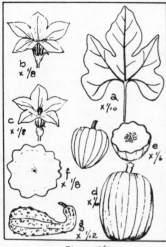

Figure 162

a, leaf; b, staminate flower; c, pistilate flower; d, field pumpkin; e, acorn "squash"; f, summer scallop "squash"; g, summer crookneck "squash."

Popular ideas are due for a startling awakening, when one studies this group. Some of the "squashes" he has been eating prove to be pumpkins and the great fruit taking the prize at the pumpkin show will most likely be a real squash. Several of our so-called squashes also fall here as shown in the illustration. The YELLOW-FLOWERED GOURDS var. ovifera with small deeply lobed leaves, and hard shelled fruit of many shapes and colors are raised for ornament or curiosity.

133b Leaves not feeling harsh or prickly; lobes pointed with
      but shallow cuts between lobes; fruit stalk hard, of
      uniform diameter except expanding as attached. Fig. 163
        CHEESE, CUSHAW AND OTHER PUMPKINS Cucurbita moschata Duch.

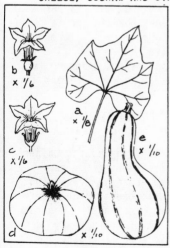

Figure 163

a, leaf; b, pistilate flower; c, staminate flower; d, Pie Pumpkin; e, Cushaw.

The plants of this species feel soft as compared to the harsh prickly plants of pepo. The Cushaws and Winter Crooknecks bear abundantly and their large solid fruit may be used in several ways much as with the preceding species. Pumpkins are often canned or dried and are sometimes made into pumpkin meal. They are frequently raised in corn fields without seeming to seriously affect the corn yield.

133c Leaves not feeling harsh or prickly; lobes rounded with shallow cuts between; fruit stalk soft, spongy, round in cross section. Fig. 164. SQUASHES Cucurbita maxima Duch.

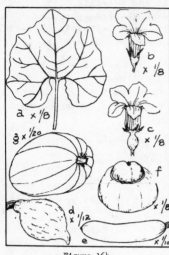

Figure 164

a, leaf; b, staminate flower; c, pistillate flower; d, Hubbard Squash; e, Banana Squash; f, Turban (Buttercup) Squash; g, Mammoth Squash.

The thickened, somewhat soft stem is one of the best characters for distinguishing these true squashes from the pumpkins. The flesh is usually an orange-yellow and firm. Squashes are particularly good for baking.

The Mammoth Squash may attain a weight of 200 pounds or more and be larger than a washtub. It must have been one of this species which "Peter, Peter, Pumpkin Eater" used for clothing his wife.

134a Sepals small, with smooth margins, not turning back towards base. 135

134b Sepals comparatively large, leaf-like, reflexed, their margins notched. Fig. 165.

CHINESE PRESERVING MELON Benincasa hispida Cogn.

Figure 165

This annual vine produces long (up to 16 inches) waxy-white fruit which is covered with hairs. The thick flesh is white and is chiefly used in preserves, although it is sometimes eaten raw. The flowers are yellow and 3 inches across. The seeds are about ½ inch long.

Other names are Zit-Kwa, Tunka, Wax Gourd and Chinese Watermelon.

Our good friends, the Chinese, have been gardening for many centuries, and have developed some very interesting and useful fruits and vegetables. Several of these have been already adopted in our country. Others are well worth trying.

135a Tendrils not branched; leaves not pinnately lobed. . . 136
135b Tendrils branched; leaves pinnately lobed. Fig. 166.
WATERMELON Vitrullus vulgaris Schrad.

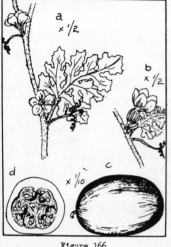

Figure 166

a, vine with staminate flowers;
b, pistillate flower; c, fruit;
d, cross section of fruit.

The watermelon is a native of
Africa and is our most popular
fruit of its type. The vines seem
rather fragile but run to some
distance and bear profusely, often
12 tons or more per acre. There
are many varieties as seen by their
shapes, colors and markings. The
flesh is usually red, though there
are yellow fleshed varieties. The
seeds may be either black or white.
The flowers are yellow. The CITRON,
a hard white-fleshed variety (var.
citroides) is used for making
preserves.

136a Fruit spiny or roughened with hard points; used green
      for pickling. 137
136b Fruit smooth or covered with slightly raised net design,
      not spiny. Fig. 167.   MUSKMELON Cucumis melo L.

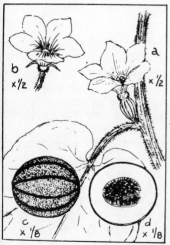

Figure 167

a, leaf and pistillate flower;
b, staminate flower; c, fruit;
d, longitudinal section of fruit.

This soft hairy vine with
angled stems, bears leaves 3 to 5
inches and yellow flowers about an
inch across. It runs to many
varieties, - NUTMEG MELONS var.
reticulatus has small fruit with
netted surface: CANTALOUPE MELONS
var. cantalupensis with hard rinds
often furrowed or rough: WINTER
MELON var. inodorus, flowers and
fruit large; keeping through winter: SNAKE MELON var. flexuosus
fruit 18-40 inches long and 1-3
inches thick: MANGO MELON var.
chito, fruit 2 or 3 inches through, flesh white used for preserves and pickles.

93

137a Leaves deeply lobed with enlarged rounded sinuses; fruit
      heavily prickeled and 2 inches or less long with many see
      Fig. 168.   BUR GHERKIN Cucumis anguria

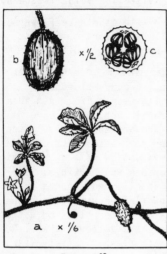

Figure 168

a, part of vine with flower and
fruit; b, fruit; c, cross section
showing seeds.

These trailing vines are rough a
with slender, angular stems. The
deeply cut leaves are about 3 inche
across. The flowers are small (1/8
to 1/2 inch), unisexual and yellow.
The very prickly fruit reaches a
length of 2 inches or less. The
fruit finds use for pickles and is
sometimes fresh boiled and eaten as
a vegetable. The term "gherkin" is
sometimes applied to certain varieties of the common Cucumber. This
plant is also known as West India
Gherkin, Gooseberry Gourd and Jamai
Cucumber.

137b Leaves scarcely lobed with sharp sinuses, if at all. Fru
      larger. Fig. 169.   CUCUMBER Cucumis sativus

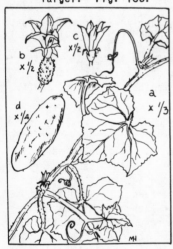

Figure 169

a, vine with leaves; b, pistilla
flower with inferior ovary (young
fruit); c, staminate flower; d, a c
cumber.

The fruit of this plant furnishe
the material for most of the pickle
used in our country. The vine is
harsh and prickly and is supplied
with tendrils for climbing, but is
usually grown in open fields where
it trails over the ground. The
bright yellow flowers measure about
1½ inches across. The fruit is usually picked while young and small.
More nearly mature cucumbers are
used for slicing and in salads.
When ripe the fruit is orange yel-
low and of but little use for food. Dill pickles are made by
natural fermentation of the cucumbers in water or brine much th
same as sauerkraut. Dill and other spices are added for their
flavor. The ENGLISH FORCING CUCUMBER var. angilicus is a coars
plant with large leaves and flowers. The fruit is slender but
may attain a length of 2 to 3 feet.

38a **Plants with one or two kinds of usually small flowers crowded into a head which is surrounded by a ring (involucre) of bracts. "Seed" an achene. Fig. 170. COMPOSITAE** 139

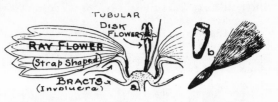

Figure 170. a, diagram of cross section of composite flower; b, achenes.

38b **Plants of various structures and many uses but apparently not as in 138a.** 144

39a **Juice milky; all flowers in the head ligulate (strap-shaped). See Fig. 170a.** 140

39b **Juice not milky; both tubular and ligulate flowers in the head. See Fig. 170a** 143

40a **Flowers blue or lavender** 141

40b **Flowers yellow. Fig. 171.   LETTUCE** Lactuca sativa **L.**

Figure 171

a, plant of head lettuce; b, leaf of leaf lettuce; c, top of fruiting stalk with flowers and seeds.

Lettuce has been much used for many years but the more recent interest in green vegetables, vitamins, etc., has greatly increased the demand for it. This annual first grows a rosette of many crisp leaves then presently a flowering stem arises to a height of 2-4 feet. Many tiny flowers with yellow rays appear in each composite head, followed, of course, by the seeds.

CURLED LETTUCE var. crispa is the home garden type, producing "leaf lettuce." HEAD LETTUCE var. capita is sold in abundance at the markets. COS and ROMAINE LETTUCE var. longifolia grow in erect-column heads. ASPARAGUS LETTUCE var. angustana, least generally known, is grown for its thick edible stems.

141a Leaves lobed and cut, often much convoluted; flowering heads sessile. L

141b Long tapering straight leaves with uncut margins; seed plume attached to seed by a peduncle. Fig. 172.

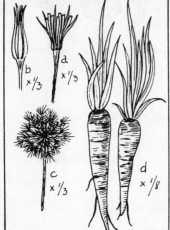

Figure 172

SALSIFY Tragopogon porrifolius

a, flowering head; b, head in bud; c, fruiting head; d, fleshy roots with leaves.

This plant, also known as Oyster Plant and Vegetable Oyster is a biennial reaching a height of some 3 feet when fruiting. The flowers are purple remaining open only during the forenoon.

The roots are white and a foot long and 2 inches thick at the top. When cooked their flavor resembles that of oysters.

It is a native of Europe.

142a Much curled leaves used for salads. Fig. 173.

ENDIVE Cichorium endivia L

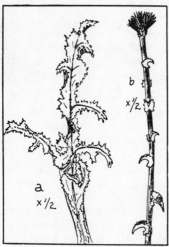

Figure 173

a, typical leaf; b, fruiting stalk with flowering head.

This plant is raised for its crisp curly leaves which are used in salads. The numerous young leaves grow in open heads and are marketed in that form. Later in the season a flowering stem arises to a height of 2 to 3 feet and produces composite heads with purple-rayed flowers.

The heads are often partly blanched by being covered for a time before cutting. It is known as "curly endive" in contrast to Witloof endive, which is a form of the next plant. It is a native of India.

"Escarole" is a broad-leaved form of Endive in which the midribs are white and heavy. It is easily blanched and is useful as a winter salad.

42b Stiff much branched plants, 1 to 3 feet high. The fleshy taproot used as a dilutant of coffee. Fig. 174.

CHICORY Cichorium intybus L.

a, fleshy roots; b, leaf; c, flowering stem with heads.

This plant has two chief food uses. The roots are sliced, thoroughly dried, roasted with a little oil, and ground, and mixed with coffee at the rate of about one ounce to a pound of coffee. It contains no caffein, but is said to make the coffee "go farther." As we write this, with coffee rationing only a day or two away, it is realized that heavy coffee drinkers may presently be wishing to try it. The roots are also put in covered trenches for forced growth. The re-sulting white leaves are eaten as

Figure 174

itloof endive. Chicory is a branching plant and grows to a eight of 3 to 5 feet, with attractive azure-blue flowers.

43a Plants 6 to 12 feet high bearing harsh opposite leaves and producing edible tubers. Fig. 175.

JERUSALEM ARTICHOKE Helianthus tuberosus L.

a, root with tubers and stem with leaves; b, branch with flowering head; c, tuber.

This is one of our native wild sunflowers. It grows to a height of 5-10 feet. The flowers are bright yellow. At its roots it produces solid club-shaped tuber sometimes reddish, others white. These tubers may be boiled, and eaten as potatoes, used in soups, or eaten raw as one eats radishes.

The food value is not high as the starch is not readily digested. Other names are Girasole and Topinambour.

Figure 175

The COMMON SUNFLOWER Helianthus annuus, a closely related plant, is frequently raised for its seed.

143b Plants 3 to 5 feet high, bearing alternate leaves and fleshy flowering heads which are prized for food. Fig. 176. **GLOBE ARTICHOKE** <u>Cynara scolymus</u> L

Figure 176

a, top of plant; b, flowering head; c, head in bud, as eaten; d, cross section of bud.

This is a coarse growing composite plant reaching a height of 3 to 5 feet. The fleshy receptacl of the large composite heads and the soft base of the bracts are th parts eaten. The flowers are purple.

The CARDOON <u>Cynara cardunculus</u> a closely related plant, is sometimes raised for its edible root and thickened leaf stalks which are blanched in the manner of celery.

Before leaving this family, the COMMON DANDELION <u>Taraxacum officinale</u> L. should be mentioned. It is a persistent European weed but much used for greens. Its flowers are a brilliant yellow and its ragged-edged leaves up to 10 inches long.

*In the preceding pages the food plants belonging to nine important families of Dicotyledons have been arranged by their natural characters. In the foregoing pages all of the food plants have been separated into groups according to their food uses. To key out a plant one may begin at number 1 on page 16, or if he prefers, here at number 144a to 144h and get the same results. It will be seen then that many plants appear at more than one place in the keys.

144h   Immature flowering buds eaten.   Fig. 177.

CAPER-BUSH   Capparis spinosa L.

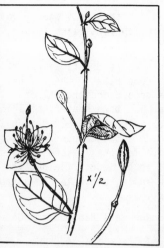

This spiny perennial shrub growing to a height of some 3 feet belongs in the warmer Mediterranean
regions, but is sometimes raised as
an annual farther north. The leaves
are 1-2 inches long. The flowers
are white and have a spread of 1½ to
2 inches with many long stamens.

The flower-buds are picked from
mid-summer until fall, dried, and
then pickeled in brine or vinegar to
which various spices are added. Before marketing the "Capers" are run
through sorting sieves to grade the
buds by size. The smaller ones are
valued most. Nasturtium fruits are
sometimes mixed with the Caper buds
to cheapen the pickles.

Figure 177

145a   Roots fleshy, tuber-like, lateral. 146
145b   Roots fibrous, but plants producing fleshy underground
       tubers 147
145c   Taproot fleshy 148
146a   Long trailing vines with morning-glory-like flowers.
       Fig. 178.   SWEET-POTATO Ipomoea batatas Lam.

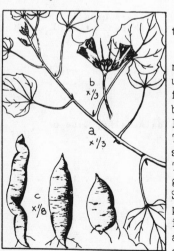

a, vine; b, flowers; sweet potatoes of different shapes.

This plant grows from thick fleshy
roots which are found rather deep
underground. The funnel-shaped
flowers, 1½ to 2 inches long are
bluish, rose-violet or pale pink.
It is a native of tropical America.
There are many cultivated varieties,
some of which are known as yams.
True yams, however, belong to the
genus Dioscorea. (See Fig. 58)
Sweet-potato plants are raised by
placing the fleshy roots in hotbeds
in early spring. Numerous sprouts
appear. These rooted young plants
are removed when 3 to 6 inches long
and set out in ridged rows. The

Figure 178

tubers continue to grow new plants, a bushel of tubers yielding
3000 to 4000 plants.

146b   Herbaceous tropical shrub to 9 feet high.   Fig. 179
          TAPIOCA-PLANT <u>Manihot</u> <u>utilissima</u> Pohl.

a, branch with deeply-lobed leaves and flowers; b, pistillate flower; c, staminate flower; d, root.

This native of Brazil is a highly important food plant. The fleshy roots are ground and the starch washed out and then heated until the starch grains explode. This mass is then made up into various forms for marketing. Tapioca is used for puddings, soups, etc. The natives grate the roots, and make bread from this plant.

Other names are Manioca and Cassava.

Figure 179

The Tapioca-plant is sometimes grown from seed, when raised commercially, but the more common practice is to plant pieces of the stem in much the same way as with Sugar-Cane. In regions subject to frost the canes are buried until spring, and are then cut into lengths of about 5 inches for planting. The roots do not keep well after being dug so they are allowed to remain in the ground until processing is ready.

147a   Herbaceous plant to 3 feet high, tubers usually smooth
          with prominent eyes, flowers star-shaped. POTATO. . 120a

147b   Sunflower-like plants 6-10 feet high; tuber usually
          hard and rough. JERUSALEM ARTICHOKE 143a

148a   Plants with milky sap; flowers daisy-like, blue or
          lavender 141

148b   Flowers not daisy-like 149

149a   Flowers with 4 separate petals, fruit a silique. . . 46

149b   Flowers with 5 petals borne in simple or compound
          umbels; fruit dry separating into two parts. 102

149c Garden or field plants with globular or elongated fleshy taproots; leaves entire or sinuate; flowers small, greenish or reddish. Fig. 180. BEET *Beta vulgaris* L.

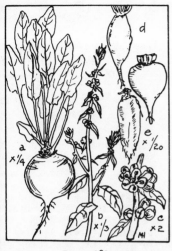

Figure 180

a, typical beet plant; b, flowering branch; c, flowers; d, root shapes; e, sugar beet.

This well known plant takes a number of forms and finds several uses. It is ordinarily a biennial and reaches a height of 2-4 feet when in bloom. The flowers are small and greenish or reddish. Table Beets are usually deep red and the roots comparatively small. Sugar Beets, on the other hand, are nearly white, often weighing several pounds each and have a sugar content of 10% or more. It is one of the world's largest sources of sugar. It is exactly the same as cane sugar with the possible exception of any scant bits of impurities peculiar to the sugar or beet plant. The leaves of beets are cooked as greens. The Mangels, large coarse growing beets, are used as stock feed.

150a Plants with composite flowers; several to many flowers united in a compact head surrounded by a whirl of bracts. 139

150b Flowers not composite 151

151a Leaves peltate (petiole attached within the margins of the blade). Fig. 181.

GARDEN NASTURTIUM *Tropaeolum majus* L.

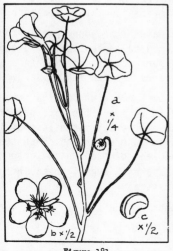

Figure 181

a, branch of plant; b, face view of flower; c, fruit.

This annual, with us, is a perennial in tropical America where it is native. The peltate leaves 2-6 inches across and the bright yellow, orange or red flowers characterize the plant. Our excuse for showing it here is the occasional use of its stems and fruit to season relishes, pickels, etc. The seeds are pickeled much the same as Caper buds. The plant is ordinarily of vining habit. *Tropaeolum tuberosum* grows irregular cone-shaped tubers 2-3 inches long which are eaten in South America.

151b Leaves not peltate. 152

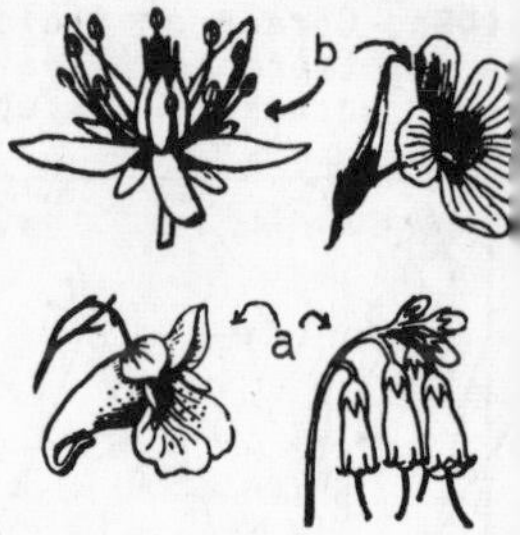

152a Flowers without petals. 156

152b Flowers with petals 153

153a Petals united into a tubular
corolla. Fig. 182a 155

Figure 182

153b Petals not united to each other. Fig. 182b. 15

154a Petals four, fruit a silique 4

154b Petals five, usually small, in compound (rarely simple)
umbels 10

154c Petals and stamens four; fruit a berry. A native of
Brazil and Paraguay. Fig. 183. MATÉ <u>Ilex</u> <u>paraguayensis</u>

a, branch of plant with fruit;
b, flower; c, section through a flow
er.

This shrubby holly plant is wide
cultivated in Brazil. It is a broa
leaved evergreen bearing clusters o
small flowers and later, red berrie

Its leaves (the young partly-gro
ones are best) are collected, dried
for 24 hours and then broken into
small pieces for tea making.

The plant contains both caffeine
and tannin in about the same propor
tions as coffee but since less of i
is used to make a serving, Maté tea
contains less of these stimulants

Figure 183

than coffee. It is served very hot and with sugar, cream or
lemon as one wishes, much as ordinary tea.

It has been long used in South America and its export to our
country has been increasing.

155a   Corolla, irregular, usually two lipped. Stems square;
       strongly flavored plants. 113
155b   Corolla regular with 5 white petals and many stamens.
       Leaves used as a beverage. Fig. 184. TEA Thea sinensis L.

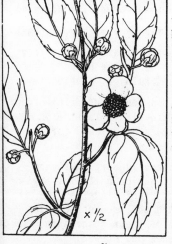

Figure 184

The use of tea as a beverage seems to date back nearly 5000 years; it has the largest use of any beverage. The plant is an evergreen shrub or tree growing to a height of 30 feet. The leaves are from 3 to 8 inches long. The white, fragrant flowers are 1 to 1½ inches across. Like most of the other important cultivated plants, it runs to many varieties. The trees are started from seed and set out permanently when quite small. They may be picked at 4 years of age. They are cut back to a height of two feet to produce quick growing shoots ("flushes") with tender leaves. The young leaves are picked by hand, then processed, sorted and packed. Black and green tea come from the same plant. In making black tea the leaves are fermented before drying.

156a   Ovary with but one cell and one seed. 157
156b   Ovary with several cells each producing one seed. Fruit
       with hard wall, indehiscent. Fig. 185.
                 NEW-ZEALAND-SPINACH Tetragonia expansa Murr.

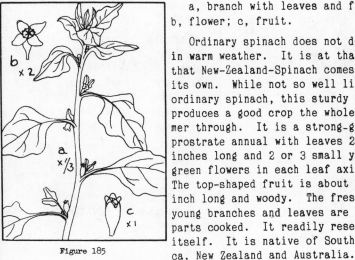

Figure 185

a, branch with leaves and fruit; b, flower; c, fruit.

Ordinary spinach does not do well in warm weather. It is at that time that New-Zealand-Spinach comes into its own. While not so well liked as ordinary spinach, this sturdy grower produces a good crop the whole summer through. It is a strong-growing, prostrate annual with leaves 2 to 5 inches long and 2 or 3 small yellow-green flowers in each leaf axil. The top-shaped fruit is about 1/3 inch long and woody. The fresh young branches and leaves are the parts cooked. It readily reseeds itself. It is native of South America, New Zealand and Australia.

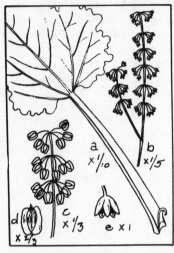

Figure 186

a, part of leaf; b, flowering branch; c, fruiting branch; d, single fruit; e, single flower.

This Old World perennial often called "Pie-Plant" is widely raised and justly famed for its acid juice.

The leaves grow from fleshy roots and may be pulled at any size. The leaf blade is discarded and the reddish petioles stripped of their outer skin, cut into pieces and stewed.

Presently a heavy flower stem arise to a height of 4-6 feet. This is usually removed early to conserve the strength to the roots. The flowers are greenish yellow followed by brown seeds.

159a Plants slender with hastate leaves. Fig. 187.
                    GARDEN SORREL Rumex acetosa L.

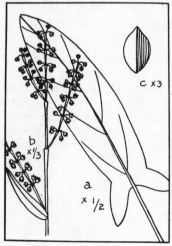

Figure 187

a, leaf; b, flowering branch; c, seed.

This plant along with others of its family, finds use as spring greens. When fruiting, it attains a height of 3 feet. Its leaves are about 5 inches long and mostly radical; with thin, light green blades and long petioles.

The yellowish-green unisexual flowers are borne on thick panicles. It is a native of Asia and Europe.

The so-called French or Belleville spinach is a variety of this species.

104

159b Plants heavier; leaves 12 to 15 inches long, not hastate.
Fig. 188.   SPINACH-DOCK Rumex patientia L.

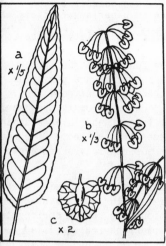

Figure 188

a, leaf; b, branch with fruit;
c, seed.

This perennial, often known as
Herb Patience, is frequently seen
growing as an escape with us.
Europe is its native home. The root
leaves are cooked as greens either
by themselves or with Spinach or
other plants. The Docks have a
pleasing acid.

Its heavy flowering panicle
rises to a height of 5 or 6 feet
and bears abundant flowers and
fruit. The leaves are usually
over a foot long and somewhat
curled.

160a Flowers perfect. Plants either with fleshy taproot or
with large petiole. 161

160b Flowers imperfect. Plants 6 inches to 2 feet high;
seeds enclosed in a more or less spiny body. Fig. 189.
SPINACH Spinacia oleracea L.

a, young plant; b, fruit;
c, fruit of Round-seeded variety.

This is the plant that gives
Popeye his prowess, and has made
martyrs of many fathers of young
children. It is a cool weather
plant, so does not do well when
warmer days are with us.

In fruit, it reaches a height
of 2 feet and has yellowish-green
flowers, followed by prickly 2 to
4 seeded fruit. ROUND-SEEDED
SPINACH var. inermis differs in
having no spines on the fruit.

ORACH Atriplex hortensis L.
is a closely related plant, oc-

Figure 189

casionally raised for similar use.

161a With fleshy, usually globular taproots; leaves as well
as root eaten. GARDEN BEET. 149

161b Petiole and midrib of leaves heavy and succulent.
Fig. 190.   SWISS CHARD Beta vulgaris var. cicla L.

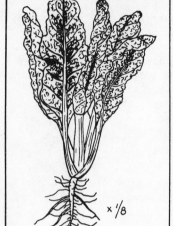

x ⅛

Figure 190

This is just a variety of the Beet
which does not have a fleshy root.
The reserve food is stored in the
leaves which possess heavy midribs
and make them prized as pot-herbs.
The plant grows vigorously from early
summer until frost and is an abundant
food producer of its kind. Some Leaf
Beets with colored leaves are grown
as ornamentals.

Seeds are produced, as with beets,
by keeping the plant over winter and
setting it out the second spring when
it will flower and fruit. It's
easier for the home gardner however
just to get them at the corner
grocery.

162a Plant yielding sugar. 163

162b Plants yielding rubber. 249

162c Plants yielding opium. Fig. 191.
OPIUM POPPY Papaver somniferum L.

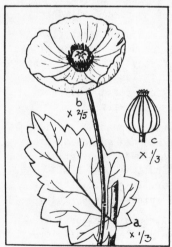

b
x ⅖

c
x ⅓

a
x ⅓

Figure 191

a, stem-leaf; b, flower; c, fruit
(capsule).

This plant likely has scant claim
to be included in a food book. It
is a usually glaucous annual 2-4 feet
high with leaves 4-10 inches long and
red or purplish flowers 3 inches or
more across. The fruit is a salt-
shaker-type of capsule.

In making opium the milky juice
from the slit capsules is collected,
dried and processed. The plant is
common with us as an ornamental.
India, Persia and China have been
the outstanding poppy raising
regions.

163a Plant producing large fleshy taproot with sweet juice.
      SUGAR BEET. 149c

163b Trees which yield sweet juice when tapped in early
      spring. Fig. 192.   MAPLES Acer spp.

a, trees tapped for sap;
b, leaves and seeds of Black Maple.

Maple sugar, once a fairly important industry, was languishing when along came sugar rationing, and this unrestricted source attained new importance. Perennials store much reserve foods in roots and stems over winter. The sap of several species of maples have a good sugar content - often 4% or better - and a pleasing flavor. Man long ago learned to tap the trees, collect the sap and by boiling out the water, to make sugar or syrup. Several species of Maple trees may be thus used. The one here pictured is Acer nigrum Michx.

Figure 192

163c Large grass-like plants with solid pith containing
      sweet juice. 164

164a Nodes (joints) far apart; grows throughout our
      country. SWEET SORGHUM. 20a

164b Nodes close together; semi-tropical or tropical.
      SUGAR CANE 19b

165a Tree; bark of roots used for beverage, flavoring and
      spring tonic. Fig. 193.
                      SASSAFRAS Sassafras albidum Nees.

a, shoot with leaves and fruit;
b, spring twig with flowers;
c, staminate flower; d, pistillate
flower; e, "mitten" leaf.

This tree may attain a height of 60 feet. The occasional two-lobed leaves have won for it the name "Mitten Tree." The flowers are small, bright yellow and appear before the leaves. The fruit is blue with red pedicels. The twigs leaves and buds are sometimes used to thicken and flavor soup. These parts, or more often the bark of the roots, are used in making "Sassafras tea."

Figure 193

107

166b Tree; bark from branches used as spice.   Fig. 194.
CINNAMON-TREE Cinnamomum zeylanicum Brey

x ⅕

Figure 194

This stiff-leaved evergreen tree grows to a possible height of 30 feet, but in cultivation is kept cu back to a few feet so that quick growing shoots are produced. These are cut when about an inch in diameter, the bark removed to loosen it, then put back in place for a few hours of fermentation. When again removed the outer part is scraped away leaving the inner bark which is then curled into a roll as stick cinnamon.

This, the original cinnamon, is produced in Ceylon. Most of the cinnamon on the market is similarly produced from the CASSIA-BARK-TREE Cinnamomum cassia, a native of China but much raised in the East Indies. The CAMPHOR-TREE is species camphora of this same genus.

166a Evergreen trees. **167**
166b Erect herbs or vines **168**
167a Tropical tree; the dried buds used for spice. Fig. 195.
CLOVE-TREE Eugenia aromatica Baill.

a, leaves, buds and flowers; b, section of flower; c, fruit.

This is a beautiful evergreen tree growing to a height of 30 feet with leaves about 3 inches long. Twice a year it produces a profusion of red or purplish flowers. The flower buds are picked and dried to furnish our cloves as they appear on the market. Cloves are now produced in the East Indies, Zanzibar and British East Africa.

ALLSPICE Pimenta officinalis Berg. a closely related 40 foot tree with white flowers, produces the small brown fruit which when dried immature, gives us this spice.

c
x½

a
x½

b
x1

Figure 195

108

167b Leaves silvery beneath; green or ripe drupe fruit pickled.
      Fig. 196.   OLIVE Olea europaea L.

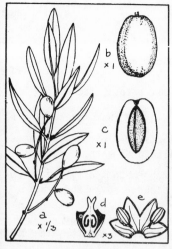

Figure 196

a, branch with fruit; b, an olive;
c, section of fruit showing seed;
d, section of pistillate flower;
e, section of staminate flower.

This is a most important tree of
25 feet or more, in the Mediterranean region and in California and Arizona. The leaves are 1-3 inches
long, densely covered with silvery
scales on under side. The flowers
are white and very fragrant. The
fruit grows to a length of ½ to 1½
inches and in shining dark purplish-
brown when ripe. The trees live to
a very old age, - perhaps as much
as 2000 years. From 10 to 30% of
the flesh of the fruit is oil, which
is rather readily extracted and
finds a good market. Both green and ripe olives are pickeled in
brine or vinegar, with or without spices.

168a Fruit a legume, flowers pea-shaped. 82
168b Leaves peltate, flowers with a spur. NASTURTIUM. . . 151a
168c Not as in 168a or 168b. 169
169a Abnormal buds or flowers developing into a fleshy
      head surrounded by cabbage-like leaves. 50
169b Fruit an elongated, five-sided capsule filled with
      shot-like seeds. Fig. 197.   OKRA Hibiscus esculentus L.

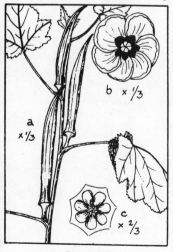

Figure 197

a, branch with fruit; b, flower;
c, cross section of fruit showing
seeds.

This plant is a near relative of
the Hollyhock and of Cotton. It
grows from 2-8 feet high. Its
large leaves may be a foot or more
across. The flowers are pale yellow with a reddish center and are
followed by elongated pods ranging
in length from 3-12 inches. These
pods have a gummy contents and are
used in soups, stews and as a
vegetable. The seeds are sometimes
roasted and used as a substitute
for coffee. Another name is
Gumbo.

169c Not as in 134a or 134b. 170

170a Sunflower-like plants producing globular flowering
heads which are eaten. GLOBE ARTICHOKE 143b

170b Trailing or climbing vines. 171

171a Fruit elongated, usually spine covered, pepo, used for
pickling. 131

171b Harsh-stemmed twining plant; fruit a soft, loose
cone-shaped body. Fig. 198.

EUROPEAN HOP Humulus lupulus L.

a, staminate flowers and leaves;
b, pistillate flowers; c, fruit.

Figure 198

This rough stemmed twining vine
with 3-5 lobed leaves and small
greenish-white flowers often grows
as an escape in our country. The
root is perennial but the vine dies
each year. The multiple fruit is
somewhat similar to that of the Mulberry to which it is related except
that each ovary is covered with a
large leaf-like bract giving the
fruit a leafy cone appearance.

Hops are used in some beverages
to impart a bitter taste and to re-
tard bacterial action. The tender
young shoots are sometimes eaten
the same as Asparagus.

The AMERICAN HOP Humulus americanus with 5-11 lobed leaves,
is similar in growth and uses.

172a Fruit a nut. 184

172b Fruit not usually considered a nut 173

173a Grass plants with narrow parallel-veined leaves. . . . 5

173b Not belonging to the grass family. 174

174a Tropical plants. 175

174b Not restricted to the tropics. 180

175a Climbing vines 176

175b Trees or shrubs. 177

176a Fleshy vine and parallel veined leaves; fruit a long
slim pod. VANILLA 33c

176b Rather woody vines; leaves net veined, fruit small ses-
      sile globular berries. Fig. 199. PEPPER Piper nigrum L.

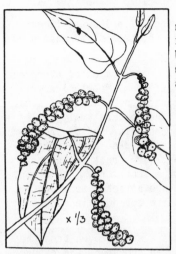

Figure 199

This tropical vining shrub is a
native of India but is cultivated
in Malaya and the East Indies. The
berries are about ¼ inch or less in
size and turn red when ripe. They
are picked and dried just before
ripening and often marketed in that
form as "whole black pepper." If
the outer covering is removed
"white pepper" results.

CUBEB Piper cubeba produces
similar berries which are used in
medicine.

This pepper plant is not at all
related or similar to the garden
peppers, Capsicum.

177a Trees 25 feet or more high. 178
177b Shrub or small tree 10-15 feet high bearing small red,
      2-seeded berries. Fig. 200.   COFFEE Coffea arabica L.

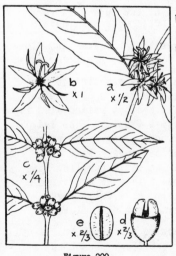

Figure 200

a, branch with flowers;
b, single flower; c, branch with
fruit; d, fruit dissected to show
seeds; e, single seed.

Coffee seems to have originated
in Abysinia and to have been prized
as a beverage for many centuries.
It is now raised in many tropical
countries with Brazil being the
largest producer. The evergreen
shrub has a height of 10 to 20
feet though in cultivation it is
trimmed back for easy picking.
The flowers are a clear white and
the pulpy berries bright red when
ripe. The pulp is removed and the
two seeds freed from a membranous
coat. Roasting is a process that
closely precedes marketing. At

least two other species of this genus are known and used in
similar way. Some fruit contain but one seed.

178a Fruit 5 inches or more in length. 179
178b Fruit less than 2 inches in length; fruit and dried
      flower buds used as spice. CLOVES. 167a

179a Fruit large, ovoid, 5 ribbed, up to 1 foot long, growing from side of trunk and larger limbs. Fig. 201.

CACAO Theobroma cacao L.

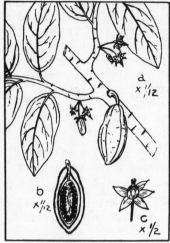

Figure 201

a, branch with leaves, flowers and fruit; b, section through a pod showing beans; c, a flower.

This 25 foot branching evergreen tree is native of Tropical America. The leaves reach a length of about a foot. The comparatively small pink flowers arise out of the stems of the tree trunks in a rather unusual way. The fruit is an ovoid pod about a foot long. The seeds, "beans," are attached to a central stem and are embedded in a soft pulp.

The beans are removed from the pods, washed, roasted, and ground in heated mills. The resulting product is the Bitter or Baking Chocolate. Much of the oil is removed to make Cocoa. Sugar and spices are added for other products.

179b Fruit 5-6 inches long. Kernels of the nuts used for drink. Fig. 202.

COLA Cola acuminata S & E.

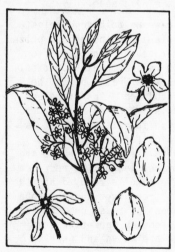

Figure 202

a, branch with leaves and flowers; b, flower; c, fruit; d, nuts.

These trees, reaching 40 feet in height are native of Tropical Africa but are now raised also in the American tropics. The leaves are 3-6 inches long. The rather small yellow flowers have no petals. One to 10 purplish nuts are enclosed in each brown pod (follicle). Five follicles usually arise from each flower.

The active principle is caffein as in Coffee. An extract from these nuts is thought to have a favorable influence on the digestive tract. It is much used in popular beverages such as Pepsi-Cola, etc.

180a   Fruit a legume.
      Fig. 203a. 82

180b   Fruit a silique.
      Fig. 203b. 52

180c   Fruit a pair of usually,
      ribbed achenes, and borne
      in compound umbels.
      Fig. 203c. 106

Figure 203. Dry fruits. a, legume; b, silique; c, Schizocarp of 2 achenes.

180d   Fruit not as in 180a, b or c 181

181a   Succulent plants with peltate leaves. NASTURTIUM. . . 151a

181b   Harsh vines with soft cone-like fruit. HOP. 171b

181c   Not as in 181a or b. 182

182a   Plants coarse with large star-shaped leaves and prickly
      fruit. Fig. 204.   CASTOR-BEAN *Ricinis communis* L.

Figure 204

a, branch with flower panicle; b, section through fruit; c, seed.

A tropical tree 40 feet high which is raised as an annual with us. Its several-lobed peltate leaves may be 3 feet across. The flowering panicles may be 2 feet high with the pistillate flowers usually at the top and the staminate ones lower on the panicle. There are several varieties varying chiefly in color. Castor-oil is made from the seeds, hydraulic presses being used to extract the oil. Quantities of this oil are used in drying cotton goods.

Other names are Palma Christi and Castor-Oil-Plant. The plant is a native of Africa, but is raised all over the world for the seed or as an ornament. The seeds are poisonous to live stock.

113

182b Field plants to 3 feet high; flowers white; fruit a three sided, sharp pointed achene. **Fig. 205.**

BUCKWHEAT Fagopyrum esculentum Gaertn.

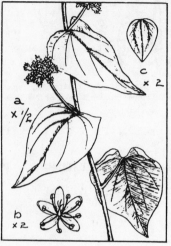

Figure 205

a, branch with leaves and flowers; b, single flower; c, three-sided seed.

This Siberian annual reached this country via Europe and is popular for making pan-cake flour. It grows to a height of 3 feet and produces a profusion of small, very sweet-scented, white flowers. The fruit is three angled and nearly black. Buckwheat flour contains more starch than that of the "small grains."

It is a favorite plant with bee raisers as it provides abundant nectar for a much prized honey.

182c Plants not as in 182a or 182b. 183

183a Annual herbs, ovary after fertilization pushes under ground, where nut develops. **PEANUT.** **84a**

183b Annual herbs raised for the fiber surrounding the seeds and for the food oil in the seeds. **COTTON** . . 241

184a Shrubs with simple leaves. **Fig. 206.**

FILBERT Corylus avellana L.

Figure 206

a, branch with fruit; b, flower catkins; c, nuts.

Several species of this genus produce closely similar nuts. They are shrubs or trees and are characterized by their long tassel-like staminate aments and the round of elongate brown nuts each borne in an enclosed husk.

The AMERICAN HAZELNUT Corylus americana grows wild in our Central and Eastern States. It gives way in our southern states to the BEAKED HAZELNUT, Corylus cornuta. The CHINESE HAZELNUT is a tree reaching a height of more than 100 feet.

114

184b Trees with simple leaves. 189
184c Trees with compound leaves. 185
185a Outer covering of fruit splitting into 4 parts. . . . 186
185b Outer covering of fruit not splitting but remaining attached to nut 187
186a Leaflets 9-17; nut cylindric. Fig. 207.
PECAN Carya pecan A. & G.

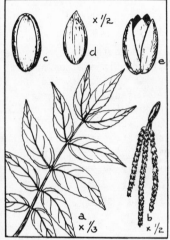

Figure 207

a, leaf; b, staminate flowers; c, fruit; d, nut; e, nut within the hulls.

This large growing hickory tree is native of the Mississippi Valley as far north as southern Iowa. In recent years it has been greatly improved by breeding, and thin shelled varieties are now extensively raised commercially. They are coming into increased uses in pastries and for other food purposes.

186b Leaflets usually 3 to 5; nut flattened on two sides. Fig. 208.
SHAGBARK HICKORY Carya ovata Koch.

Figure 208

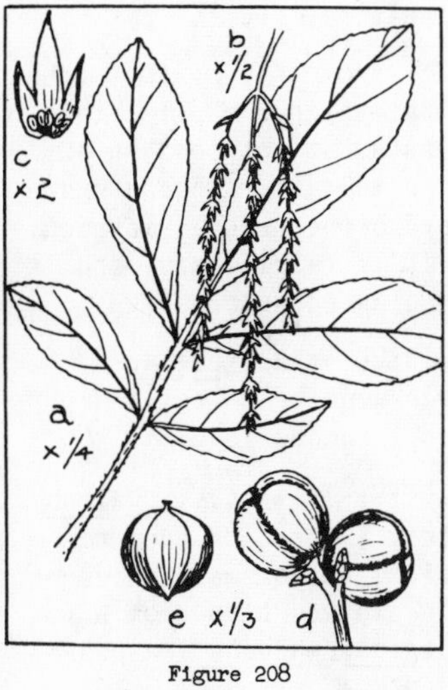

a, leaf; b, staminate ament; c, single staminate flower; d, fruit; e, nut.

This common forest tree, reaching a height of 120 feet, often produces quantities of hard shelled nuts of exceptionally good flavor. They and the nuts of several other similar species are gathered in the fall for home consumption or to put on the market.

The BIG SHELLBARK HICKORY grows nuts often more than an inch in length. The shell however is so thick and convoluted that it is difficult to remove the meat. The nuts of several species such as the Bitternut and Pignut are too bitter to be edible.

187a Leaflets serrate; young twigs pubescent. Nuts rough
      and thick shelled. 188

187b Leaflets almost entire; twigs glabrous. Nuts thin
      shelled and fairly smooth. Fig. 209.
                          ENGLISH WALNUT Juglans regia L.

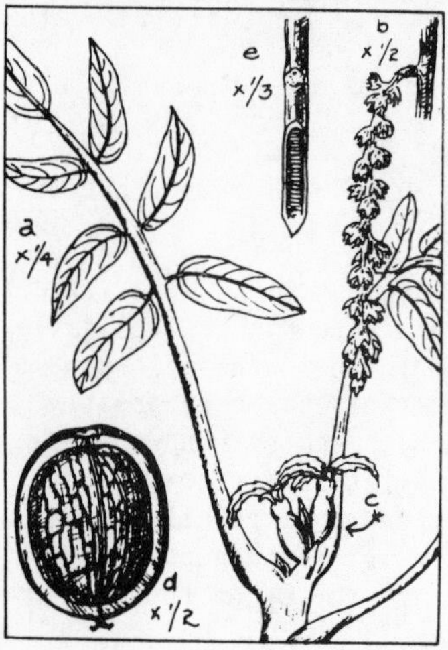

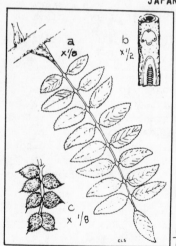

a, stem and leaves; b, staminate
flowers; c, pistilate flowers;
d, fruit with nut exposed; e, stem
showing pith.

A native of South-eastern Europe
and China, this thin shelled nut is
much raised in California and has a
good market demand. The trees
reach a height of 50 feet or more.
The nuts are permitted to fall or
are "polled" off, removed from the
hull, cleaned, bleached and sorted
before being put on the market.

Improved strains are perpetuated
by grafting and budding.

Figure 209

188a Fruit in long racemes covered with vicid hairs. Leaflets
II-17, densely serrate. Fig. 210.
                      JAPAN WALNUT Juglans sieboldiana Maxim.

a, leaf; b, stem showing pith,
and leaf scar; c, fruit.

The nuts from this 60 foot tree
are somewhat thinner shelled than
Black Walnuts but not so thin as
the English Walnuts. The nuts are
pointed and borne several in each
raceme. It is fairly hardy and is
sometimes planted with us.

The CHINESE WALNUT Juglans
cathayensis also bears pointed
nuts about 2 inches long.

The CALIFORNIA WALNUT, Juglans
californica, a shrub or tree to
60 feet high, bears small pubescent
fruit. The leaves have from 9 to

Figure 210

17 leaflets. A MANCHURIAN WALNUT, Juglans mandshurica produces fruit two inches or more in length.

116

188b Fruit solitary or in pairs, almost spherical. Leaflets 15
      to 23. Bark of larger limbs, dark and rough. Fig. 211.
                              BLACK WALNUT Juglans nigra L.

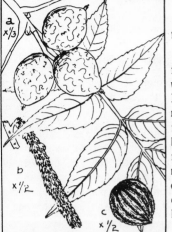

a, leaf and fruit; b, staminate
flowers; c, nut.

This great 150 foot tree is of
first importance because of its fine
wood for furniture and other uses.
Its nuts, however, have a distinctive
much-liked flavor and are gathered
for home use and market sale. The
hull contains a penetrating and
rather permanent brown strain, which
marks the young walnut collectors
each fall. The crank-turned type of
corn-sheller offers a quick means of
hulling the nuts.

Figure 211

188c Fruit elongate, in clusters of 3 to 5, coated with rust-
      colored sticky hairs. Leaflets 11 to 17. Bark of larger
      limbs with smooth light areas. Fig. 212.
                              BUTTERNUT Juglans cinerea L.

a, leaf; b, staminate ament;
c, winter twig, showing leaf-scars;
d, fruit; e, nut.

This tree is often called "White
Walnut," presumably in reference to
its light colored heart wood. The
bark has smooth light patches in
contrast to the rough dark bark of
the Black Walnut. The leaves have
from 11 to 17 leaflets and they
and the fruit are covered with a
sticky pubescence.

The nut meats are not as bulky
as those of the Black Walnut and
more difficult to get out of the
shell. If the nuts are held on
end when cracked, the meats may

Figure 212

usually be gotten out much better.

188d Tropical or sub-tropical; fruit a drupe, the seed known
      as PISTACHIO-NUT. 231a

117

189a Native American trees; fruit a prickly nut; leaves with
one fairly large simple serrate tooth for each lateral
vein, in which it ends 190

189b Not as in 189a 191

190a Leaves with slender points on the teeth often incurving.
Leaves more than twice as long as wide, green on both
sides. Bark rough. Fig. 213.

CHESTNUT <u>Castanea dentata</u> Borkh.

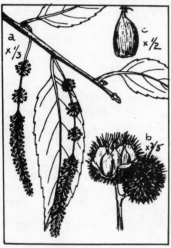

a, branch with staminate flowers;
b, fruit (burs) with nuts; c, chestnut.

This native American tree grows
to a height of 100 feet and has
leaves 10 inches long. Its 2-3 nuts
are grown in a very prickly bur
which breaks open in the fall and
pours out the nuts. They are one
inch or less across.

The CHINQUIPIN is another native
species which bears similar but
smaller nuts of excellent flavor.
Foreign Chestnuts are the Eurasian,
Chinese and Japanese, all of which
have nuts larger, but inferior in
flavor to our American species.

Figure 213

190b Leaves without slender points at tips; usually less than
twice as long as wide. Bark smooth, light gray. Several
3-sided nuts borne in the spiny fruit. Fig. 214.

BEECH <u>Fagus grandifolia</u> Ehrh.

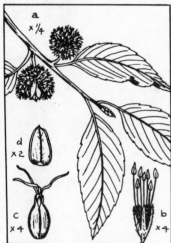

a, branch with leaves and fruit;
b, staminate flower; c, pistillate
flower; d, seed.

Beech nuts grow in very prickly
burs much the same as chestnuts;
the nuts however are three angled
and smaller. They would appear to
be overgrown buckwheat grains.
Their sweet-flavored kernels give
them good food value. The tree
grows to a height of 100 feet and
has smooth light gray bark and
beautiful lustrous green foliage.
The EUROPEAN BEECH, <u>Fagus sylvati-
ca</u> is often planted with us as an
ornamental. The nuts are similar
to those already described.

Figure 214

118

191a Trees peach-like, fruit a drupe, its fleshy covering
      splitting early. The seed constitutes the "nut."
      ALMOND. 72b

191b Not peach-tree-like 192

192a Receptacle becoming fleshy and forming the largest part
      of the fruit; supporting a curved nut at its end.
      Fig. 215.   CASHEW Anacardium occidentale L.

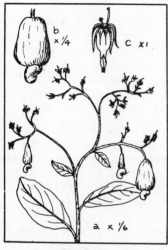

Figure 215

a, branch bearing flowers and fruit; b, fruit; c, flower.

This 40 foot, wide-spreading tropical evergreen yields both fruit and nuts in the same package. A large fleshy pear-shaped body with pleasing acid pulp is first on the pedicel; then at its apical end, as though Nature just noticed that the seed had been forgotten, is attached the familiar cashew nut. The "cashew-apple" turns red or yellow when ripe. It is 2 to 4 inches in length and is eaten raw or used for beverages and other foods. The nuts are eaten both raw and roasted, but when raw must be handled with care for within the shell is a caustic blistering liquid which heat dispels. The flowers are yellowish-pink and about ½ inch long.

192b Receptacle normal. 193

193a Fruit a woody shelled spherical ball 3 to 6 inches in
      diameter enclosing several close fitting 3 sided nuts.
      Fig. 216.   BRAZIL NUT Bertholletia
                                    excelsa H. & B.

Figure 216

a, flowering branch with leaves; b, fruit cut open to show nuts; c, typical nut; d, kernel from nut.

This 150 foot tree, native of northern South America, is scarcely known outside its own region except by its nuts. The leaves are leathery and about 2 feet long; the flowers are cream colored and the spherical fruit, with thick woody wall, reaches 6 inches in diameter. The fruit wall is broken with difficulty. Inside are 18 to 24 triangular nuts, each with one large fleshy kernal, in taste resembling that of the coconut.

119

193b Fruit not as in 161a. 194

194a Fruit 5 inches or more long containing several to many
      seeds 179

194b Fruit about 2 inches; single brown seed covered with
      scarlet net-like covering. Fig. 217.

                    NUTMEG Myristica fragrans Hout.

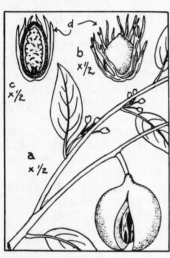

a, branch with leaves, flowers
and fruit (flesh cracking to expose
nut); b, nut surrounded by aril
(mace); c, section through nut;
d, covering of nut (mace).

This tree, a native of the East
Indies, may attain a height of 60
feet or more, but the trees in cultivation are usually kept cut back
to about 25 feet. The leaves are
2-5 inches long, the flowers are
inconspicuous and the fruit yellowish or reddish, up to 2 inches
in diameter. The outer fleshy
covering is removed; under it and
surrounding the nut is a scarlet
lacework which is dried and marketed as the spice, Mace.

Figure 217

The nuts are dried until the kernel shrinks away from the
enclosing shell, which is then removed. This dry kernel is
the Nutmeg used as a spice in cooking.

195a Fruit a berry (pulpy; arising from one pistil, and
      having few to many seeds). Fig. 218a 196

195b Fruit a drupe (fleshy, with the
      usually but one seed enclosed in a
      stony endocarp). Fig. 218b 227

195c Fruit a syncarp (many druplets
      arising from separate flowers but
      united into one fruiting body).
      Fig. 218c 235

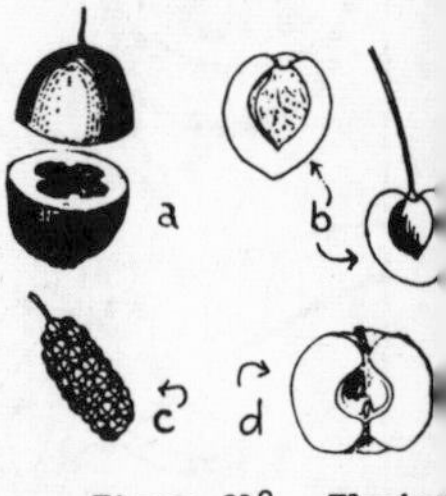

Figure 218. Fleshy
fruit types. a, berry
b, drupes; c, syncarp;

195d Fruit a pome (as in the apple).
      Fig. 218d 77

d, pome.

196a Plants with thick expanded leaf-like stems belonging to
the Cactus family.   Fig. 219.

INDIAN-FIG Opuntia ficus-indica Mill.

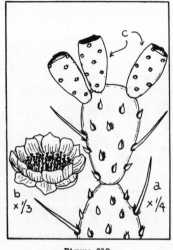

Figure 219

a, part of plant with fruit;
b, flower; c, "pears."

Over 1000 species of the Cactus
family are known. All are of
American origin, although they have
been carried to all parts of the
world. All they possess in the way
of leaves are some tiny scale-like
structures, the parts generally as-
sumed as being leaves are truly
stems. The fruit of the species,
here pictured, is from 2 to 4
inches long and usually yellowish
when ripe with the interior red.
The pulpy contents is quite sweet
and is intermingled with large
seeds. This fruit is much depended
on in Mexico and other regions.

The TUNA Opuntia tuna is another species the fruit of which
is much used.

The flowers are yellow, and the fruit of the different
species and varieties ranges in color from yellow to reds and
purple.

198d Stemless plants with trifoliate leaves; spreading by
      runners. STRAWBERRIES. 61b

199a Plants hairy or prickly with alternate leaves and
      fruit a pepo. CUCURBITAE 131

199b Plants glabrous; stamens united in a tube and surrounding
      the stalk of the ovary. Stem sometimes somewhat woody.
      Fig. 220.   WILD PASSION-FLOWER Passiflora incarnata L.

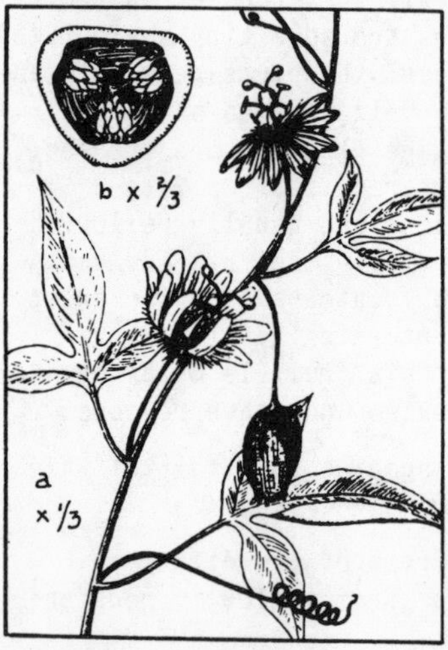

Figure 220

a, vine with flower and fruit;
b, cross section of fruit.

This climbing vine, native of our
southern states may attain a length
of 30 feet. The leaves are 3-5
inches long and the white flowers
with purple crown about 2 inches
across. The fruit becomes about
the size of an egg and yellow when
ripe.

The GRANADILLA Passiflora
edulis, a Brazilian species with
deep purple fruit 2-3 inches long,
is widely cultivated in sub-
tropical regions. A number of
other similar species are edible.

    The fruit is eaten raw or used in cooking and baking, and
has a pleasing flavor.

200a Petals not united. Fig. 221a. 205

200b Petals united. Fig. 221b. 201

201a Flowers unisexual. Staminate flowers long tubular,
      yellow with 10 stamens on
      throat, sepals small
      (pistilate flowers with
      distinct petals) PAPAYA. . . 212b

201b Both stamens and pistils in
      the same flower. Fig. 221. . 202

202a With but one style 203

Figure 221. a, petals separate
b, petals united.

202b Styles two or more. **Fig. 222.**

PERSIMMON Diospyros virginiana L.

Figure 222

a, branch with fruit; b, flower.

This tree reaches a forest height of 50 feet or more, with leaves some 6 inches long; the fruit is yellowish or pinkish-orange when ripe and may be 1½ inches in diameter though usually smaller. It is exceedingly astringent when green, but becomes sweet, mild and delicious when fully ripened, frost or no frost, current opinion not-with-standing.

The JAPANESE PERSIMMON, Diospyros kaki bears orange or reddish fruit to 3 inches in diameter with excellent flavored orange-colored flesh; often appears in the markets.

Ebony wood comes from the heart of a tree of this genus.

203a Flowers with sterile stamens (sometimes resembling petals). 204
203b Flowers with 5 fertile and no sterile stamens; fruit 2-4 inches in diameter, purple or light green, Fig. 223. STAR-APPLE Chrysophyllum cainito L.

Figure 223

a, branch with fruit; b, cross section through fruit showing seeds.

This tropical evergreen tree with 6 inch shining leaves grows to a height of 50 feet or more. The flowers are purplish-white and the spherical fruit which is about 4 inches in diameter is greenish to purple. The pulp is pinkish-white rather translucent and contains up to 8 brown seeds.

Many such tropical fruits are delightful but must be tree ripened and are poor keepers. With the coming of common air-freight we should see many of them on the markets in our temperate regions.

204a Sterile stamens petal-like, fruit rusty-brown, flesh yel-
low-brown. Fig. 224. SAPODILLA Sapota achras Mill

Figure 224

a, tree trunk groved for collecting chicle; b, fruit; c, cross section of fruit showing seeds.

This widely distributed tropical
evergreen tree reaching 75 feet has
two distinct uses. The milky sap is
collected, boiled down and becomes
the base (chicle) for most all of
our chewing gums. It is interesting
to note that the first use of chicle
was for making rubber.

The 3 inch fruit with a rough
yellowish-brown skin and translucent
flesh of similar color with large
shining black seeds is truly delicious. The flowers spread ½ inch
and are white.

204b Sterile stamens only filaments, fruit orange-yellow,
flesh orange-like. Fig. 225.

CANISTEL Lucuma nervosa A. DC.

Figure 225

a, branch with fruit; b, cross
section through fruit, showing
seeds.

This slender tree 25 feet high
with greenish-white flowers comes
from tropical South America. Its
leaves are bright green and 4 to
8 inches long. The fruit has
flesh like an orange and orange
colored. They are from 2-4
inches in diameter. Other names
are Egg-Fruit and Ti-es.

205a Stamens more than 10 and more than twice as many as
the petals. 206

205b Stamens usually 5 or 10 but never more than twice as
many as the petals. 212

206a Calyx attached to the ovary, leaves punctate. . . . 207

206b Calyx not attached to the ovary; a very large tree; fruit covered with dense hair. Fig. 226.
                    BAOBAB Adansonia digitata L.

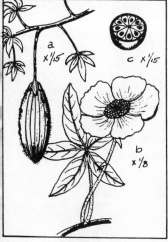

Figure 226

a, branch with fruit; b, flower; c, cross section of fruit.

This great African tree is also known as Monkey Bread and Sour Gourd, and is said to have the thickest trunk of any known tree although its height is only around 60 feet. It apparently grows to great age.

The fibrous bark is used for making clothes and rope while the acid-pulp fruit is eaten. The leaves when dried and powdered are used for seasoning.

The flowers are white and 6 inches or more across. Their stems are sometimes 3 feet long.

207a Ovary usually 1-3 celled. 209

207b Ovary usually 4 to 5 celled, stamens not much longer than the petals 208

208a Young stems with four angles; veins of leaves con- spicuous. Fig. 227.   GUAVA Psidium guajava L.

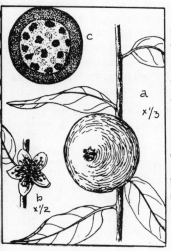

Figure 227

a, branch with leaves and fruit; b, flower; c, cross section of fruit.

Guavas grow on shrubs or small trees and while native of Tropical America are raised in the warmer parts of our Southern States. The fruit varies from spherical to pear shape and when ripe is yellow or red. Guavas are prized for jellies, preserves, jams, etc., but are not very good to be eaten uncooked. The fruit ranges from 1 to 4 inches in length.

The flowers are white and about 1 inch across.

208b Young stems round in cross section; veins not prominent.
      Fig. 228.   **STRAWBERRY GUAVA** _Psidium cattleianum_ Sabine

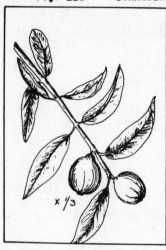

This fruit is smaller and with
less flavor than the Guava but
never-the-less is a favorite for
jelly and jams in some regions. It
grows on a shrub or small tree.
The 1 inch flowers are white. The
fruit 1 to 1½ inches in diameter,
is purplish-red with white flesh.
One variety has bright yellow fruit.
It is native of Brazil.

There are other species of
Guavas, but not so well known as
the two pictured.

Figure 228

209a Ovules hanging from tip of cell. Berry dark brown about
      ¼ inch in diameter. Fig. 229.
                         ALLSPICE _Pimenta officinalis_ Berg.

a, branch with fruit; b, panicle
of flowers; c, flower.

This forty foot tree is a native
of the West Indies and Central
America. The leathery leaves are 6
to 7 inches long. The ¼ inch white
flowers are borne in panicles. The
berries that follow are picked before ripening and sundried. Since
their flavor seems to resemble a
mixture of several spices they have
been called "Allspice."

Other names are Pimento and
Jamaica Pepper.

The BAY-RUM TREE _Pimenta acris_
is a similar and closely related

Figure 229

tree. It is the leaves in its case which yield the product.

209b Ovules not as in 209a. 210

210a With 3 to many flowers on each peduncle. 211

210b But one flower on each peduncle (though several pe-
      duncles may arise at the same place). Often a shrub.
      Fig. 230.   PITANGA Eugenia uniflora L.

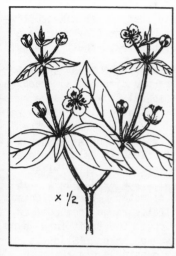

The fruit of this 25 foot shrub
or tree is a crimson 1 or 2 seeded
spicy-flavored berry nearly an inch
in diameter. Its home is Brazil
and Argentina. The fragrant flowers are about ½ inch across and
white. Another name is Surinam-
cherry.

The JAMBOLAN Eugenia jambolana
is a somewhat larger tree with
small flowers and the branches
white. Its half-inch berries are
purplish-red. It belongs in the
East Indies.

x ½

Figure 230

211a Flowers ¼ inch across, light-purple. CLOVE TREE. . 167a

211b Flowers 2 to 4 inches in diameter, greenish-white.
      Fig. 231.   ROSE-APPLE Eugenia jambos L.

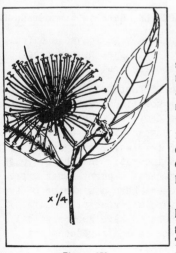

Here is another tropical evergreen tree, - in this case only 30
feet high. It is native of the
East Indies but is grown in our
southern areas chiefly as an ornamental. The flowers are 3 inches
across with many conspicuous stamens and are greenish-white. The
fruit is yellow and about 2 inches
in diameter. Its flesh is rather
dry and lacking in taste when
eaten fresh, but is prized for
preserves.

The AUSTRALIAN BUSH-CHERRY,
Eugenia myrtifolia, is frequently
grown as a hedge in warm regions.
The 1 inch long red or purplish
fruit is used in jellies.

x ¼

Figure 231

127

212a Leaves simple, entire, glandular punctate; fruit
      globose, solid. 213
212b Leaves up to 2 feet across, blades as broad as long
      and much cut; fruit hollow with many spherical seeds.
      Fig. 232.   PAPAYA Carica papaya L.

a, young tree with fruit;
b, single leaf; c, staminate flower; d, pistillate flower; e, section through fruit showing seeds.

This herbaceous plant grows to
tree form and dimensions, reaching
25 feet in height with leaves sometimes 2 feet across. The pale yellow flowers are imperfect. The
fruit roughly resembles a musk mel-
lon. The flesh is salmon colored
and the cavity is filled with
spherical black seeds about 3/16
inch in diameter. The more common
market fruits range from 6 to 12
inches long. The fruit is enjoyed
both raw and cooked. Since it

Figure 232   contains papain, a digestant acting as pepsin, the Papaya is the more popular.

213a Fruit when mature pale yellow (sometimes greenish) to
      red-orange; flowers when fully open, white.
      RUTACEAE. 93
213b Fruit reddish-purple; flowers 2 inches across, rose-pink;
      leaves 6 to 10 inches long. Fig. 233.
                      MANGOSTEEN Garcina mangostana L.

a, branch with leaves and fruit;
b, fruit with part of covering removed showing fruit sections.

This 30 foot Malayan tree bears
what is sometimes said to be the
world's choicest fruit. The
fruit, shaped like an orange, contains 5 to 7 white segments and a
few small seeds. The thick, tough
rind is reddish-purple when ripe.
The flowers have a diameter of two
inches and are rose-pink. It
would seem to have good possibilities once it is introduced into
our markets.

Figure 233

216a Orange sized globular fruit filled with seeds each of
      which is surrounded by its own juicy pulp. Fig. 234.

POMEGRANATE Punica granatum L.

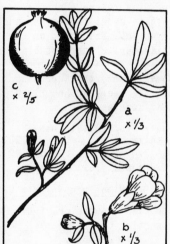

a, branch with leaves; b, bud and flower; c, fruit.

This shrub (rarely a tree) grows to a possible height of 20 feet. The flowers are orange-red and waxy. The globular fruit 1½ to 4 inches in diameter contains several cells. Its many seeds are surrounded by a thick reddish, acid pulp. The fruit varies in color from pale yellow to pink, red and purplish-red.

Its chief use is in beverages and is more appreciated in hot dry climates. It has a long history but is not particularly popular.

Figure 234

Its quantity of seeds seem to be against it. A dwarf variety is raised as a pot plant.

Variety nana is a dwarf form popular for pot culture. Double flowered varieties and others with different color shades are raised as ornamentals.

216b Aromatic woody shrubs or trees not as in 216a.
      Family MYRTACEAE. 207

217a Leaves pinnately compound.
      Fig. 235a. 218

217b Leaves simple. Fig. 235b. . 219

Figure 235. a, pinnately
compound leaf; b, simple leaf.

218a Fruit aggregate (a collec-
      tion of drupelets). BRAMBLES 62

218b   Fruit a 4-celled berry about ¼ inch in diameter. Fig. 236.
       ELDERBERRY Sambucus canadensis L.

Figure 236

a, branch with fruit; b, single flower.

Several somewhat similar species of Elders are known. This one, known as the American or Sweet Elder is widely scattered east of the Rockies and its fruit was much used by early settlers and is still in use because of its flavor. The bushes grow to a height of 10 or 12 feet. The flowers are borne in wide spreading umbel-like cymes and are cream white. The fruit up to ¼ inch in diameter is purplish-black and is borne in great profusion. The European Elder, the European Red Elder, the American Red Elder and the Blue Elder are somewhat similar species.

219a   Petals separate, on throat of calyx tube; fruit many
       seeded crowned with remains of calyx. 220
219b   Petals united 222
220a   Stems with spines at nodes, flowers and fruit in groups
       of usually 1-4.   Fig. 237.
       GARDEN GOOSEBERRY Ribes grossularia L.

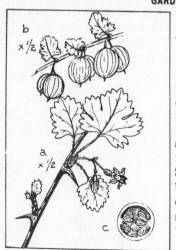

Figure 237

a, stem with flowers; b, fruit; c, cross section of fruit.

This is the European Gooseberry, the one generally planted for garden use. It is a shrub reaching a height of 2 to 5 feet. The berries may be an inch or more in length but are usually smaller and are very sour until ripened. The flowers are greenish or yellowish. Several species of native gooseberries grow wild throughout our country and their fruit is often gathered and used. They are sometimes cultivated.

Gooseberries are used green more often than when ripe. They are alike in having thorns at the nodes and some species have prickles on the fruit.

220b Stems without spines at nodes, flowers and fruit in
      racemes. CURRANTS. 221

221a Fruit black; leaves resinous-dotted. Fig. 238.
                          BLACK CURRANT Ribes nigrum L.

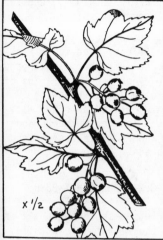

x 1/2

Figure 238

This is the European Black Currant, a sturdy bush growing to a height of 5 feet or more, the fruit of which is used for jellies, preserves and the like. The flowers are greenish-white and the fruit is black.

The AMERICAN BLACK CURRANT Ribes americanum grows wild and bears similar fruit but it has an unpleasant flavor. Several varieties of Ribes nigrum are grown. They differ in the color of the ripened fruit and in the shape of the leaves. The MISSOURI or BUFFALO CURRANT Ribes aureum is planted for its golden yellow sweet scented flowers. One variety is grown for its fruit.

221b Fruit red or white (sometimes striped); leaves not dotted.
      Fig. 239.   COMMON CURRANT Ribes sativum Syme.

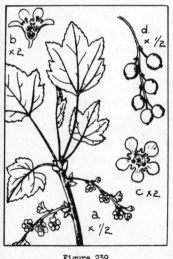

b x2

d x 1/2

c x2

a x 1/2

Figure 239

a, branch with flowers; b, section through flower; c, face view of flower; d, fruit.

This European shrub, common in many gardens, grows to a height of 3-5 feet. It bears many small greenish, yellowish or purplish flowers in hanging racemes. The fruit is a bright red or in some varieties, white. Currants are often used in cooking while still green. Currants are especially prized for jellies. Several other European and native currants are known but are little planted with us. Small seedless grapes when dried and used in baking are often referred to as "currants."

222a Stamens free from the corolla, leaves alternate;
      berries bluish-black or red. 223

222b Stamens attached to the corolla, leaves opposite, plants to 12 feet high; scarlet berries borne on cymes. Fig. 240.
HIGH CRANBERRY **Viburnum trilobum** Marsh.

a, branch with fruit; b, section through flower; c, fruit.

This vigorous shrub may reach a height of 12 feet. The white flowers are borne in rather flat-topped umbel-like cymes, the outer ring of which has sterile flowers with large sepals, while the other flowers are much less conspicuous and fertile. The fruit is scarlet and eaten by birds. It is used for jellies, etc.

The EUROPEAN CRANBERRY-BUSH, often seen is quite similar. One of its varieties is the Snowball in which all the flowers are sterile, and then, of course, bears no fruit.

Figure 240

The BLACK-HAW Viburnum prunifolium has bluish-black fruit with large flat disk-like seeds. It is frequently eaten.

223a Fruit bluish-black with white bloom; flowers cylindrical; anthers not extending out of corolla. **224**
223b Fruit red, flowers 4-parted, open; anthers extending out of corolla. Fig. 241.
AMERICAN CRANBERRY **Vaccinium macrocarpon** Ait.

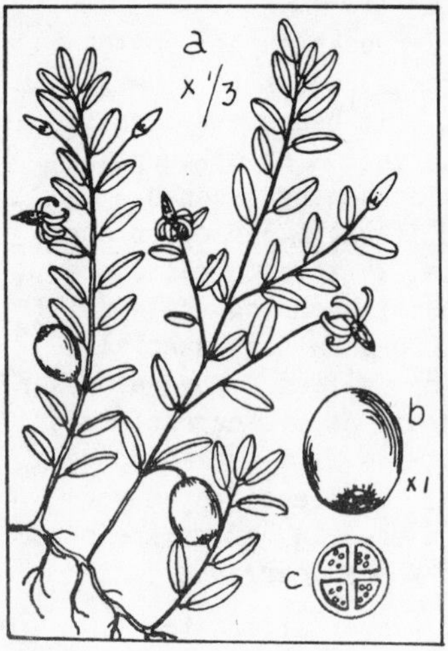

a, branch with leaves, flowers and fruit; b, single cranberry; c, cross section of fruit.

This woody evergreen has somewhat creeping stems 3 feet long. The leaves are less than an inch long and whitish beneath. The flowers are pink and about 1/3 inch across. The red fruit may be round, oval or pear shaped and is usually around ¾ inch long.

Cranberries are raised in bogs which can be flooded at will. They are usually picked by use of comb-like scoops.

Figure 241

The EUROPEAN CRANBERRY Vaccinium oxycoccus, a similar plant but smaller and bearing smaller fruit is sometimes raised.

132

224a   Plants 4 to 12 feet high, flowers pinkish or white.
Fig. 242.   HIGH-BUSH BLUEBERRY Vaccinium corymbosum L.

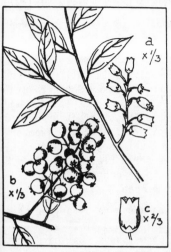

Figure 242

a, branch with leaves and flowers; b, fruit; c, single flower.

The shrubs may reach a height of 12 feet or more with leaves 3 inches long. The flowers are bell shaped about 1/3 inch long, pale pinkish. The bluish-black fruit is covered with a whitish bloom and is about 1/3 inch in diameter. It is later in fruiting than our other Blueberries.

WINTERGREEN Gaultheria procumbens L. used for flavoring is a closely related plant.

There seems to be much confusion in the use of such names as Blueberry, Huckleberry, Whortleberry and Billberry. Other apparently good names for this plant are Swamp Blueberry and Huckleberry.

224b   Plants seldom over 2 feet high; flowers greenish-white.
Fig. 243.   LOW BLUEBERRY Vaccinum pennsylvanicum Lam.

Figure 243

a, branch with fruit; b, flowering branch; c, single flower.

This somewhat prostrate little shrub grows to a length of 6 inches to 2 feet. The flowers are about ¼ inch long and the bluish-black fruit which is usually covered with a bloom is ¼ to 3/8 inch in size. It is among the first to ripen. Blueberries are often picked by use of a comb-scoop like that used with Cranberries.

Other similar plants whose fruit has food uses are HAIRY HUCKLEBERRY Vaccinium hirsutum native of Georgia and North Carolina, WHORTLEBERRY Vaccinium myrtillus, a Eurasian species with black fruit, and BLACK HUCKLEBERRY, Gaylussacia baccata a 3 foot deciduous shrub with black fruit.

225a   Tropical vine; leaves broad, ovate, entire; fruit ¼ inch in diameter or less, yellowish-red. PEPPER. 176b

133

225b Tendril-climbing woody vines, leaves palmately lobed. . 2
226a Tendrils forked and intermittent (absent from each third
      node). Fig. 244.   VINIFERA GRAPE Vitis vinifera

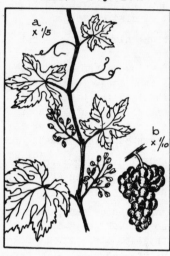

Figure 244

a, portion of vine with flower
buds; b, fruit.

This European grape is now raise
very extensively in California and
some extent in other Southern State
An aphid, the Grape Phylloxera and
mildew rule it out of other regions
These Vinifera grapes are sweeter
than our American grapes and always
favorites for table. The skin adhe
to the pulp in contrast to most
American grapes.

Raisins are made by drying these
grapes, and from a small seedless
variety comes the so-called dried
currants used in baking.

There are many different varie-
ties; one var. apiifolia with much dissected leaves is raised a
an ornamental.

226b Tendrils forked and continuous (at practically every node
      bunches with many berries). Fig. 245.
                         LABRUSCAN GRAPES Vitis labruscana Bailey

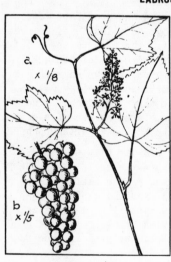

Figure 245

a, branch with leaves and inflorescence; b, fruit.

America has several species of
wild grapes. Some of these have
been improved by selection and
crossing with each other and with
the European grape until there are
many rather widely differing
varieties.

The Concord, derived from the
above species, is likely the best
known and most widely raised east
of the Rockies. Its fruit is purplish-black with a whitish bloom.
The flowers are small and greenish
yellow. Their petals fall as the
buds open.

Other varieties derived from this species take various
shades of greenish-white and red when ripe. They do not keep
on ship as well as the Vinifera grape.

134

226c Tendrils not branching. Fig. 246.
MUSCADINE GRAPE <u>Vitis</u> <u>rotundifolia</u> Michx.

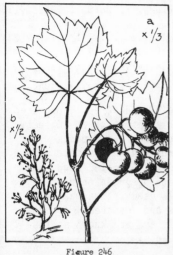

Figure 246

a, leaves and fruit; b, panicle of flowers.

The Muscadine is a southern grape. It has been broken into several varieties by cultivation and selection. The leaves are 2 to 6 inches across and smooth. The fruit is borne in small bunches of a very few to rarely 15 or 20 berries each, often ½ to 1 inch in diameter.

"Scuppernong," a favorite variety bears fruit that when ripe is reddish-brown though often flecked with green. It is prized more for cooking and jellies than as a table grape.

The RIVERBANK GRAPE <u>Vitis</u> <u>vulpina</u> is a common wild species the small black acid fruit of which is in strong favor for jellies.

227a Palm tree bearing its elongated drupe-like fruit in
      great clusters. DATE PALM. 10b
227b Not a palm. 228
228a Native American shrub to 18 feet high, leaves 2 inches
      long, silvery both sides, drupes ½ inch, red or yellow.
      Fig. 247.   BUFFALO-BERRY <u>Shepherdia</u> <u>argentea</u> Nutt.

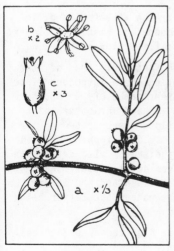

Figure 247

a, branch with fruit; b, staminate flower; c, pistillate flower.

This thorny 10-18 foot shrub is a native of the North and West. The young branches and leaves are matted with silvery hairs. The yellowish flowers are followed by little globular drupes that are red when ripe (var. <u>xanthocarpa</u> has yellow fruit). It is a very hardy shrub and is often employed for an attractive hedge.

The berries in earlier times were served as a sauce with buffalo meat which likely accounts for the name. They are prized for jelly making and are sometimes dried for winter use.

231a   Leaves odd pinnate with 3 to 11 leaflets; flowers
brownish green; drupe, 1 inch long, reddish. Fig. 248.
                                PISTACHIO <u>Pistacia</u> <u>vera</u> L.

Figure 248

This spreading deciduous tree attains a height of 25-30 feet. The flowers are dioecious. The wrinkled reddish fruit is valued for its thin-shelled seed, the yellowish or greenish meat of which is used in the making of candies and ice cream, or eaten directly and are known as Pistachio Nuts.

The tree is raised in ways similar to the Olive and in the same regions.

231b   Leaves even pinnate with 2 to 4 pairs of leaflets. . **232**

232a   Surface of fruit smooth, green; flowers greenish-white.
Fig. 249.
                      SPANISH-LIME <u>Melicocca</u> <u>bijuga</u> L.

Figure 249

a, branch with fruit; b, inflorescence; c, staminate flower; d, pistillate flower.

This West India tree of some 60 feet has been introduced into the warmer areas of our southern states. The fragrant greenish-white flowers are borne in panicles. The drupe is about 1 inch in diameter with green skin and translucent yellow flesh. Both the flesh and the large seed are eaten, the latter being roasted.

It is also known as Mamoncello and Genip.

232b Surface of fruit roughened with tubercles, bright red. Fig. 250.

LITCHI Litchi chinensis Sonn.

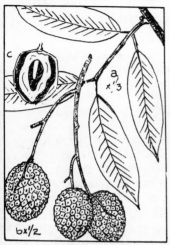

Figure 250

a, compound leaf; b, fruit; c, section through dried fruit.

This famous Chinese fruit or nut is now grown in many warmer regions. The round topped tree reaches a height of 30 feet or more, the small greenish-white flowers are followed by a thin brittle shelled globular fruit which becomes a bright red upon ripening. The flesh is translucent, pinkish-white, sweet and aromatic.

The fruit is eaten fresh, used in preserves and dried as a confection. The tubercule covered shell of the dried "nuts" is a rust brown.

233a Fruit globose 4-6 inches in diameter, russet, flowers white, I inch. Fig. 251.

MAMMEE-APPLE Mammea americana L.

Figure 251

a, branch with leaves; b, fruit.

This beautiful tree of some 60 feet grows in tropical South America and the West Indies. The leathery leaves are a glossy green like many tropical evergreens. The white flowers are 1 inch across and fragrant. The globular fruit may attain a diameter of six inches. It has 1-4 large seeds imbedded in its bright yellow flesh. The somewhat roughened russet skin is bitter but the flesh is delightful either raw or in preserves. Its flavor has given it another name of South American Apricot.

The tropics have many delicious fruits most of which can be grown only in frost free areas and many of which can not be kept long when removed from the plant on which they grew.

233b Fruit variable shaped 2-6 inches long, greenish, yellowish or reddish; leaves 6-16 inches long. Fig. 252.

MANGO Mangifera indica L.

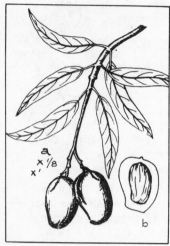

Figure 252

a, branch with fruit; b, fruit sectioned to show seed.

Likely of Asiatic origin, the Mango justly famed for its delicious fruit is wildly grown in tropical and near-tropical areas. The tree is a beautiful broad-spreading evergreen nearly 100 feet high. The small pinkish-white flowers are borne in terminal panicles. The fruit varies in size from 2 to 6 inches and may be globular or elongated and yellow-green or red when ripe.

There are good and bad Mangos, the difference being much in the relative size of the seed and the quantity of fibers attached to it.

233c Fruit pear-shaped or globose 2 to 9 inches long, surface roughened, green or purple. Fig. 253.

AVOCADO Persea americana Mill.

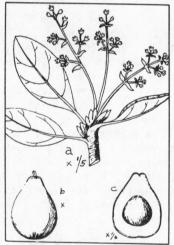

Figure 253

a, flowers and leaves; b, fruit; c, section of fruit showing seed.

This evergreen tree comes from Tropical America. It is very sensitive to frost which greatly limits the areas where it may be grown. The small greenish flowers are born in panicles. The fruit which attains a length of 2 to 9 inches may be spherical or pear shaped. The color when ripe is usually green or purple though there are brown and red varieties.

The one large seed is surrounded by an oily pulp which is counted delicious by many.

The MEXICAN AVOCADO Persea drymifolia has anise-scented leaves and smaller fruit.

233d Fruit smaller than 233 a, b, or c. **234**
234a Drupe ½ to 1½ inch long, black when ripe; leaves 1-3 inches long, green above, silvery beneath.
OLIVE. **167b**

234b   Drupe 1½ to 2 inches long, dark red or brown, whitish
       flesh. Tree or shrub; leaves 1-3 inches long, green.
       Fig. 254.   JUJUBE Zizyphus jujuba Mill.

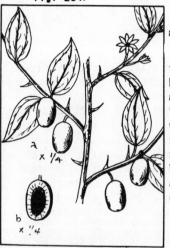

a, branch with leaves, flowers
and fruit; b, section showing seed.

This evergreen shrub or small
tree to 30 feet is raised in the
Mediterranean region and in Asia,
also in California and Florida.
The small flowers are whitish
while the ½ to 2 inch long fruit
ranges in color from yellow to
red brown and in some varieties
black. It is used much the same
as prunes or dates. The sugar
content is high.

Figure 254

235a   Vine with leaves two feet broad, much punctured; fruit
       stands erect 6-12 inches (a monocotyledon) CERIMON. . . 30b
235b   Low growing plant with long spear-shaped leaves; fruit
       3-10 inches long in center (a monocotyledon) PINEAPPLE. 33a
235c   Not as in 235a or b 236
236a   Flowers having no petals. Trees. 237
236b   Flowers with 6 petals. Calyx 3 parted. Trees. 238
237a   Fruit 4-8 inches in diameter; leaves 18 to 30 inches
       long. Fig. 255.   BREAD-FRUIT Artocarpus communis Forst.

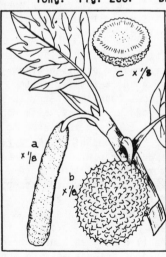

a, staminate spike; b, fruit;
c, cross section of fruit.

This tropical tree attains a
height of 60 feet. The large
globular fruit is covered with
prickles and is yellow when ripe.
Its contents is starchy and it is
usually cooked as a vegetable while
still green.

The natives make many uses of
it. The leaves are unusually
large.

The Jackfruit Artocarpus
integra is a somewhat similar 70
foot tree. Its club shaped fruit
may be 2 feet long.

Figure 255

139

237b   Flowers concealed within a pear-shaped receptacle which ripens to become the fruit.   Fig. 256.

COMMON FIG   Ficus carica L.

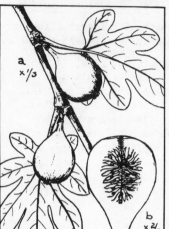

Figure 256

a, branch with leaves and fruit; b, section through fruit.

The fig is a peculiar plant in that its small flowers are always hidden within the fleshy receptacle which becomes the fruit. It is often said, it does not have flowers but that is a mistake. The tiny wasps which pollinate the plant must crawl into the small opening at the end of the receptacle with their load of pollen or the many seeds which make the fig appreciated would not develop. The tree may reach a height of 30 feet. The fruit is not a good keeper so while dried, preserved and canned figs are common, fresh ones do not travel far in quantities. It might seem from its early choice that the fig should also be included in the "wearing" section. It seems however that its use as clothing did not last long.

237c   Fruit resembling a blackberry ½ to 1 inch long.   Fig. 257.

WHITE MULBERRY   Morus alba L.

Figure 257

a, branch with fruit; b, fruit in detail; c, fruit of only one flower; d, catkin of pistillate flowers; e, staminate flowers.

This Chinese "white" mulberry usually bears red or purplish-black fruit, though occasionally white. It is the most common mulberry in many parts of our country, although its fruit is inferior in flavor to our native RED MULBERRY Morus rubra. The White Mulberry is used for feeding silkworms but functions more largely with us in providing acceptable food for our native birds. The BLACK MULBERRY Morus nigra, a European favorite for its fruit, is sometimes grown here. The fruit coarsely resembles blackberries but is derived from many flowers instead of but one as with the blackberry.

140

238a Leaves velvety beneath.

Fig. 258.
CHERIMOYA Annona cherimola Mill.

x ¹/₅

Figure 258

Ecuador and Peru have given this delightful fruit to the subtropics. The deciduous tree grows to a height of 25 feet; its leaves 10 inches long and its fragrant yellow to brownish flowers an inch across. The juicy fruit has a greenish exterior with white pulp and grows from apple size to specimens weighing 15 pounds. There are several varieties that differ in the shape of the fruit and type of surface.

The SOURSOP Annona muricata, a 20 foot evergreen of Tropical America is closely related and bears similar fruit.

238b Leaves smooth beneath; carpels in fruit but loosely
      united. Fig. 259.

SUGAR-APPLE Annona squamosa L.

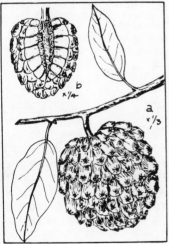

b
x¹/₄

a
x¹/₃

Figure 259

a, leaves and fruit; b, section through fruit.

This is another deciduous tree reaching a height of 20 feet and producing yellowish-green fruit about three inches in diameter. The flowers are greenish-yellow and about an inch long. It comes from Tropical America. The fruit is eaten both raw and cooked. Another name is Sweetsop.

The CUSTARD-APPLE Annona reticulata bearing heart-shaped reddish or brownish fruit up to 5 inches in diameter is similar.

THE PLANTS WE WEAR*

241a   Seeds with extra long fibers (lint) but without a short
woolly covering (smooth when lint is removed at the gin).
Flowers bright yellow with purplish tinge. Many of the
leaves 5-lobed. Fig. 260.

SEA-ISLAND COTTON Gossypium barbadense L.

a, plant with flower and boll;
b, seed with fiber; c, seed as it
comes from the gin.

This cotton plant grows to a
height of 3-8 feet. The natives of
the West Indies were using it when
Europeans first visited the islands.
The lint is finer and longer (1 3/8-
2 inches) than that of Upland Cotton,
so brings a considerably better
price, but its yield is less and the
cost of harvesting more. It is now
raised along the coast of Georgia
and Florida as well as in several of
the West India Islands.

Figure 260

*A few of these are Monocotyledons and have already been pictured and described there,
but we include them in this key to make the list more complete. At best the number
of plants thus used is surprisingly small. Of course, man draws as further sources
for wearing apparel on the animals and in a smaller way on the minerals. Skins, furs,
wool and other hairs, feathers and silk contribute in large ways. A list of the
animals commonly supplying materials for our clothing, would not be large. The ad
writers give us many names of furs, for instance, but literally hundreds of these come
from the back of the lowly rabbit. Sheep and silkworms furnish a large percentage of
our clothing materials.

241b Seeds with shorter fibers, and covered with short woolly hairs after ginning; flowers white or pale yellow turning pink or purplish. Leaves 3-lobed. Fig. 261.

UPLAND COTTON Gossypium hirsutum L.

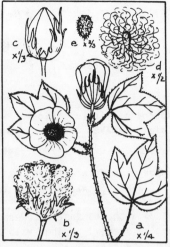

a, branch with flower; b, open boll ready to pick; c, mature boll; d, seed with lint; e, seed as it comes from the gin.

This is the type of cotton most extensively raised and used in our country. Originally it was a perennial in the tropics but is now raised as an annual, growing to a possible height of 5 feet.

The fruit or "boll" contains a number of seeds, each covered with a long lint; when cotton ripens the bolls split open exposing the fiber. After picking, done by hand or machines, the cotton is ginned, to separate the fiber

Figure 261

from the seeds. The seeds - in this species covered with a short fuzz - are used for one of our most important food-oils, and for cattle feed and fertilizer.

241c Leaves with rounded tips. Fig. 262.

INDIAN COTTON Gossypium herbaceum L.

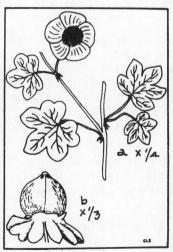

a, leaves and flowers; b, fruit (boll).

This is the species of cotton most largely grown in China and Southern Asia. It is a smaller and weaker plant than either of the other two species described. The flowers are yellow with purple center; the seeds are large and angled. The lint is coarse and short and ranges in color from white to yellow and golden brown. Several other species of cotton are cultivated. PERUVIAN COTTON Gossypium peruvianum is grown in Peru and Brazil. TREE COTTON Gossypium arboreum is raised in Asia and Africa. It grows to a

Figure 262

height of 10 feet with dark reddish-purple flowers.

242a Banana-like plants, the leaves of which supply
       fibers. . . . . 33▶

242b Palm-like plants the leaves of which produce fans and
       fibers. CHINESE FAN PALM . . . . 9▶

242c Plants with long sword-like leaves arising in whorls
       from the ground or near it. 243

243a Bearing a large fleshy multiple fruit at center.
       Fibers from leaves used for fine "pina-cloth."
       PINEAPPLE 33a

243b Leaves thick and fleshy; the source of fibers. Flow-
       ers and dry fruit on tall panicles. AGAVES 31a

244a Leaves simple 245

244b Leaves alternate, palmately compound, plants 3 to 12
       feet high. Fig. 263.   HEMP Cannabis sativa L.

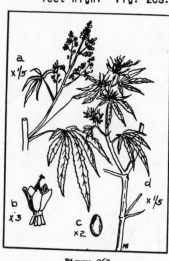

Figure 263

a, branch with staminate flowers;
b, flower; c, seed; d, branch with
pistillate flowers.

This rather attractive annual
plant may grow to a height of 20
feet. It is of Asiatic origin but
is widely raised for its tough stem
fibers. It is known to have been
used as a fiber plant for 3000 years
or more.

The leaves are palmately compound
and attain a length of some 9 inches
The greenish-yellow staminate flowers are borne in panicles often a
foot high. The pistillate flowers
are greenish and grow in leafy
spikes on separate plants from the
staminate flowers.

The plants are cut green and "retted" in water to free the
fibers much the same as is practiced with flax for which it is
substituted. Plans are under way to raise greatly increased
acreages of hemp in our country.

The fruit is a small globular achene which is used in
poultry feed and mixed in canary bird seed.

The plant is often seen growing as an "escape."

245a   Leaves about ½ as wide as long with serrate margins. . 246

245b   Slender branching annual I to 4 feet high; leaves small,
      linear, entire. Fig. 264.   FLAX   Linum usitatissimum L.

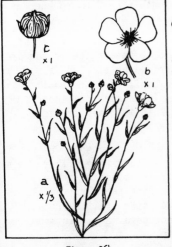

a, part of plant; b, flower;
c, dry capsule containing the seeds.

This herbaceous annual growing to
a height of 2-3 feet is a dual purpose plant, one variety being raised
for its seed from which linseed oil
is made, and the other for its
fibers which are used for producing
linen. The plants are cut very
close to the ground (pulled in primitive culture) cleaned of its seed
and dried. The straw is then "retted"
by soaking in water for a few weeks
or by spreading out on the ground to
take the dew and rain. This is to
loosen the fibers which are removed,
cleaned, bleached, spun and woven.

Figure 264

The flowers are a beautiful azure blue.

NEW ZEALAND FLAX Phormium tenax, a member of the lily family,
furnishes fibers for cords and ropes.

246a   Herb or shrub 3 to 6 feet high, much branched.   Flower
      small. Fig. 265.   RAMIE   Boehmeria nivea Goud.

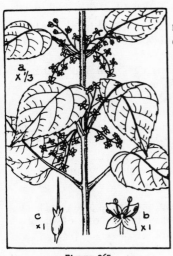

a, portion of plant with staminate flower; b, staminate flower;
c, pistillate flower.

This herb or shrub, also known
as Chinese Silk Plant is much
raised in China and India where it
is native, and also in some warmer
parts of Europe and America. Its
height is about 6 feet. It has
unisexual flowers, both types of
which are borne on the same plant.
The leaves have a white felt-like
undersurface. The fibers are removed from the stem and used to
make a beautiful silk-like cloth
as well as cord and paper. It is
very strong, not readily affected

Figure 265

by moisture and takes dye well.

Chinese Grass Cloth is made from these fibers. While a member of the nettle family it does not have stinging hairs.

246b Annual to 15 feet high, branching only near top. Flowers yellow, stamens many. Fig. 266.

JUTE Corchorus capsularis L

a, branch with flowers and fruit b, flower; c, fruit.

This vigorous annual reaches a height of 15 feet. The leaves are characterized by ear-like basal teeth. The flowers are small and yellow. It is much raised in India and somewhat in other tropical countries.

The fibers are removed by retting as with flax and hemp. They are not as strong as either of these and deteriate more rapidly. Jute cloth, twine and paper are its products. Burlap for bags, etc., is made from Jute.

Figure 266

NALTA JUTE Corchorus olitorius, distinguished from its near relative by the elongated fruit has the same uses.

247a Fleshy roots ground to fine powder for use as a dye. Leaves whorled in 4's to 6's, flowers greenish-yellow. Fig. 267.

MADDER Rubia tinctorum L.

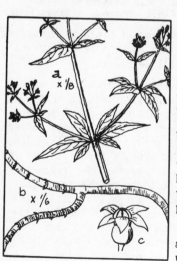

a, branch with leaves and flowers; b, piece of root; c, flower.

This plant which grows to a height of 4 feet has whorled leaves up to 4 inches long. The flowers are yellowish-green and rather inconspicuous. The fruit, a small fleshy berry is at first red and becomes black when ripe. The long fleshy roots are dried and ground to a very fine powder from which a highly permanent red dye is obtained. It has been largely replaced by synthetic dyes.

This plant found uses with the ancient Egyptians, one of which was coloring the wrappings of mummies.

Figure 267

247b Leaves used to make henna dye. Shrub to 20 feet; flowers very fragrant, white to red. Fig. 268.

HENNA Lawsonia inermis L.

Figure 268

a, branch with panicle of flowers; b, single flower; c, fruit capsule; d, seeds.

This shrub of tree growing to a height of 20 feet is valued as an ornamental as well as furnishing a dye "worn" on nails and hair. Its small but very fragrant flowers are borne in conspicuous panicles. The flowers range in color from white to rose and cinnabar-red. The flowers are similar to the Crape-Myrtle one of the most attractive shrubs in our southern states. The leaves and flowers are used to make Henna dye.

247c Nectar from large greenish-yellow flowers used for making perfume. Tree to 80 feet high; leaves 8 inches long. Fig. 269.

YLANG-YLANG Cananga odorata H. & T.

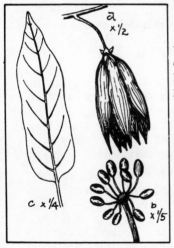

Figure 269

a, flower; b, fruit; c, leaf.

The very fragrant flowers of this tropical tree are the source of a famous perfume. It reaches a height of 80 feet. The greenish-yellow flowers are about 2 inches long and the many-seeded fruit is one inch long and colored green. It is a native of the Phillipines, East Indies and Southern Asia but is grown in Florida.

The CLIMBING YLANG-YLANG Artabotrys odoratissimus also known as "Tail-Grape" is a climbing tropical evergreen with similar flowers and fruit.

248b Sap used to make guttapercha. Fig. 270.
GUTTAPERCHA TREE Palaquium gutta Burck.

× ⅓

Figure 270

This evergree Malayan tree grows to a height of 40 feet. Its milky sap is collected by removing alternate strips of bark from the trunk and taking the sap as it exudes. It is prepared much as with rubber making, but lack the elasticity of that product. It makes a good insulater and waterproofer.

The leaves are about 4 inches long and covered with a dense rusty pubescence below, the flowers inconspicuous and the fruit a small fleshy berry.

249a Tall trees with simple leaves 5 to 12 inches long.
Fig. 271.   ASSAM RUBBER-TREE Ficus elastica Roxb.

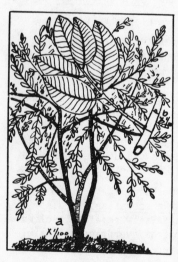

a
× ¹⁄₁₀₀

Figure 271

a, tree; b, leaves.

This relative of the Common Fig is a native of Malaya and was one of the first sources of rubber. In its native region it often starts as an epiphyte but overgrows the tree on which it develops and becomes a rather sizable tree on its own. This is the rubber plant commonly raised as a pot-ornamental.

Its thick milky sap is collected and coagulated into rawrubber. The leaves are 5 to 12 inches long and leathery. The flowers are inconspicuous, with fruit yellowish-green and about ½ inch long.

"Rubber" is today one of the hardest words in the English language. "Of all sad words of tongue or pen, the saddest are these 'It might have been.'"

148

249b   Tree to 60 feet with compound leaves (3 leaflets).
Fig. 272.   PARA RUBBER-TREE   Hevea brasiliensis Muell.

Figure 272

a, tree; b, leaves and fruit.

This is our chief source of rubber, a major contribution to our joys and more recent grief.

It is a native of the Amazon valley but is raised most extensively in Malaya and the East Indies. The tree attains a height of 60 feet, has leaves up to 2 feet long, white flowers and a woody fruit bearing 3 large seeds.

The milky juice or latex is secured by tapping the trees after they are six years old. Trees of this age and with much work of daily tapping and collecting produce about one pound of rubber per year - somewhere near the amount lost when a truck skids once.

Many plants have sap from which rubber could be made. A few that are so employed with some success are

MEXICAN RUBBER-TREE Castilla elastica a 60 foot tree with leaves 12-20 inches long.

CEARA RUBBER Manihot glaziovii a Brazilian 40 foot tree.

SILK RUBBER Funtumia elastica a very large tree not producing until 20 years old.

WEST AFRICAN RUBBER Landolphia spp. Several species of climbing plants.

PLANTS WE EAT AND WEAR

ARRANGED IN THEIR BOTANICAL ORDER

ust as maps show the connections of towns and countries so an arrangement of plants in their logical order serves to shed a new light on their relationship and significance. All the plants commonly eaten or used in clothing are arranged below by their botanical groups and families for convenient reference.

Check the list. How many of these plants could you recognize at sight? How many of them have you used for food? An interesting and profitable game for some social gathering could be built around that.

DIVISION THALLOPHYTA

ALGAE

Agar-Agar.	Gelidium cartilagineum Gaill. P. 17
Irish Moss	Chondrus crispus Stac. P. 17
	Gigartina mammillosa

LICHENS

Iceland Moss	Cetaria islandica Ach. P. 18

FUNGI

Yeast.	Saccharomyces cerevisiae Han. P. 16
Common Morel	Morchella esculenta Pers. P. 18
Common Mushroom.	Agaricus campestris L. P. 19

DIVISION SPERMATOPHYTA

MONOCOTYLEDONS

GRASS FAMILY Gramineae

Pod Corn	Zea mays tunicata St. Hil. P. 23
Pop Corn	Zea mays everta Bailey.ᵗ P. 23
Flint Corn	Zea mays indurata Bailey. P. 25
Dent Corn.	Zea mays indentata Bailey. P. 25
Soft Corn.	Zea mays amylacea. P. 24
Sweet Corn	Zea mays rugosa Bonaf. P. 24
Job's Tears.	Coix lacryma-jobi L. P. 26
Sweet Sorghum.	Holcus sorghum saccharatus Bailey. P. 27
Broom-Corn	Holcus sorghum technicus Bailey. P. 28
Durra.	Holcus sorghum durra Bailey. P. 28
Kafir.	Holcus sorghum cafforum Bailey. P. 27
Sugar-Cane	Saccharum officinarum L. P. 26

Broom-Corn Millet. . . . . . Panicum milliaceum L.   P. 29
Pearl Millet . . . . Pennisetum glaucum R. Br.   P. 29
Foxtail Millet . . . . Setaria italica Beauv.   P. 30
Rice . . . . Oryza sativa L.   P. 30
Oats . . . . Avena sativa L.   P. 31
Wheat. . . . . Triticum aestivum L.   P. 32
Rye. . . . . Secale cereale L.   P. 32
Barley . . . . Hordeum vulgare L.   P. 31

PALM FAMILY Palmaceae

Chinese Fan Palm . . . . . . Livistona chinensis R. Br.   P. 20
Coconut Palm . . . . Cocos nucifera L.   P. 21
Date Palm. . . . . Phoenix dactylifera L.   P. 21

ARUM FAMILY Araceae

Taro. Dasheen. . . . . . . Colocasia esculenta Schott.   P. 33
Ceriman. . . . . Monstera delicosa Liebm.   P. 33

PINEAPPLE FAMILY Bromeliaceae

Pineapple. . . . . Ananas comosus Merr.   P. 35

LILY FAMILY Liliaceae

Garlic . . . . Allium sativum L.   P. 37
Leek . . . . Allium porrum L.   P. 36
Welsh Onion. . . . . Allium fistulosum L.   P. 39
Onion. . . . . Allium cepa L.   P. 38
Shallot. . . . . Allium ascalonicum L.   P. 38
Chive. . . . . Allium schoenoprasum L.   P. 37
Garden Asparagus . . . . . Asparagus officinalis L.   P. 34
New Zealand Flax . . . . . Phormium tenax Forst.   P. 146

AMARYLLIS FAMILY Amaryllidaceae

Agaves . . . . Agave spp.   P. 34

YAM FAMILY Dioscoreaceae

Chinese Yam. . . . . Dioscorea batatas Decne.   P. 39
Yellow Yam . . . . Dioscorea cayennensis L.   P. 39
Cush-Cush. . . . . Dioscorea trifida L. f.   P. 39
Air Potato . . . . Dioscorea bulbifera L.   P. 39

BANANA FAMILY Muscaceae

Banana . . . . Musa paradisica sapientum L.   P. 35
Abaca. . . . . Musa textilis Nee.   P. 35

GINGER FAMILY Zingiberaceae

Common Ginger . . . . . . Zingiber officinale Rosc.   P. 40

ARROWROOT FAMILY Marantaceae

Arrowroot. . . . . Maranta arundinaceae L. P. 40

ORCHID FAMILY Orchidaceae

Common Vanilla . . . . . . Vanilla planifolia Andr. P. 36

DICOTYLEDONS

PEPPER FAMILY Piperaceae

Pepper . . . . Piper nigrum L. P. 111
Cubeb. . . . . Piper cubeba L. f. P. 111

WALNUT FAMILY Juglandaceae

English Walnut . . . . . . Juglans regia L. P. 116
Black Walnut . . . . Juglans nigra L. P. 117
Butternut. . . . . Juglans cinerea L. P. 117
Japan Walnut . . . . Juglans sieboldiana Maxim. P. 116
Chinese Walnut . . . . . . Juglans cathayensis. P. 116
Pecan. . . . . Carya pecan A & G. P. 115
Shagbark Hickory . . . . . Carya ovata Koch. P. 115

BIRCH FAMILY Betulaceae

Filbert. . . . . Corylus avellana L. P. 114
American Hazelnut. . . . . Corylus americana Walt. P. 114

BEECH FAMILY Fagaceae

Chestnut . . . . Castanea dentata Bor. P. 118
Beech. . . . . Fagus grandifolia Ehrh. P. 118
European Beech . . . . . . Fagus sylvatica L. P. 118

MULBERRY FAMILY Moraceae

White Mulberry . . . . . . Morus alba L. P. 140
Red Mulberry . . . . Morus rubra L. P. 140
Black Mulberry . . . . . . Morus nigra L. P. 140
Bread-Fruit. . . . . Artocarpus communis Forst. P. 139
Common Fig . . . . Ficus carica L. P. 140
Assam Rubber-Tree. . . . . Ficus elastica Roxb. P. 148
Mexican Rubber-Tree. . . . Castilla elastica. P. 149
Hemp . . . . Cannabis sativa L. P. 144
European Hop . . . . Humulus lupulus L. P. 110
American Hop . . . . Humulus americanus Nutt. P. 110

NETTLE FAMILY Urticaceae

Ramie. . . . . Boehmeria nivea Gaud. P. 145

BUCKWHEAT FAMILY Polygonaceae

Buckwheat. . . . . Fagopyrum esculentum Gaertn. P. 114
Garden Rhubarb . . . . . . Rheum rhaponticum L. P. 104

Garden Sorrel. . . . . . . Rumex acetosa L. P. 104
Spinach-Dock . . . . Rumex patientia L. P. 105

GOOSEFOOT FAMILY Chenopodiaceae

Beet . . . . Beta vulgaris L. P. 101
Swiss Chard. . . . . Beta vulgaris cicla L. P. 106
Spinach. . . . . Spinacia oleracea L. P. 105
Orach. . . . . Atriplex hortensis L. P. 105

CARPET-WEED FAMILY Aizoaceae

New-Zealand-Spinach. . . . Tetragonia expansa Murr. P. 103

CUSTARD-APPLE FAMILY Annonaceae

Soursop. . . . . Annona muricata L. P. 141
Cherimoya. . . . . Annona cherimola Mill. P. 141
Sugar-Apple. . . . . Annona squamosa L. P. 141
Custard-Apple. . . . . . . Annona reticulata L. P. 141
Ylang-Ylang. . . . . Cananga odorata H & T. P. 147
Climbing Ylang-Ylang . . . Artabotrys odoratissimus R. Br. P. 147

NUTMEG FAMILY Myristicaceae

Nutmeg . . . . Myristica fragrans Hout. P. 120

LAUREL FAMILY Lauraceae

Sassafras. . . . . Sassafras albidum Nees. P. 107
Avocado. . . . . Persea americana Mill. P. 138
Mexican Avocado. . . . . . Persea drymifolia C & S. P. 138
Cinnamon-Tree. . . . . . . Cinnamomum zeylanicum Breyn. P. 108
Cassia-Bark-Tree . . . . . Cinnamomum cassia Blume. P. 108

POPPY FAMILY Papaveraceae

Opium Poppy. . . . . Papaver somniferum L. P. 106

CAPER FAMILY Capparidaceae

Caper-Bush . . . . Capparis spinosa L. P. 99

MUSTARD FAMILY Cruciferae

Cabbage. . . . . Brassica oleracea capitata L. P. 46
Brussels Sprouts . . . . . Brassica oleracea gemmifera Zenker. P. 47
Cauliflower. . . . . Brassica oleracea botrytis L. P. 44
Asparagus or
    Sprouting Broccoli. . . Brassica oleracea italica Plenck. P. 44
Kales. Borecole. . . . . . Brassica oleracea acephala DC. P. 49
Kohlrabi . . . . Brassica caulorapa Pasq. P. 41
Rutabaga . . . . Brassica napobrassica Mill. P. 43
Turnip . . . . Brassica rapa L. P. 43
Leaf Mustard . . . . Brassica juncea Cass. P. 45
Pe-tsai or Chinese Cabbage Brassica pekinensis Rupr. P. 46

Pak-choi. . . . . Brassica chinensis L. P. 46
False Pak-choi. . . . . . . Brassica parachinensis Bailey. P. 46
Black Mustard . . . . Brassica nigra Koch. P. 45
Winter-Cress. . . . . Barbarea vulgaris R. Br. P. 49
Upland-Cress. . . . . Barbarea verna Asch. P. 49
Water-Cress . . . . Roripa nasturtium-aquaticum Hayek. P. 48
Bitter-Cress. . . . . Cardamine pratensis L. P. 48
Horse Radish. . . . . Armoracia rusticana Gaertn. P. 42
Garden Cress. . . . . Lepidium sativum L. P. 48
Garden Radish . . . . Raphanus sativus L. P. 42
Sea-Kale. . . . . Crambe maritima L. P. 47

SAXIFRAGE FAMILY Saxifragaceae

Common Currant. . . . . . . Ribes sativum Syme. P. 131
Black Currant . . . . Ribes nigrum L. P. 131
American Black Currant. . . Ribes americanum Mill. P. 131
Buffalo Currant . . . . . . Ribes aureum Pursh. P. 131
Garden Gooseberry . . . . . Ribes grossularia L. P. 130

ROSE FAMILY Rosaceae

Strawberry. . . . . Fragaria chiloensis ananassa Bailey. P. 5
Everbearing Strawberry. . . Fragaria vesca L. P. 50
Salmonberry . . . . Rubus spectabilis Pursh. P. 51
Blackcap Raspberry. . . . . Rubus occidentalis L. P. 51
Red Raspberry . . . . Rubus idaeus L. P. 52
Purple Raspberry. . . . . . Rubus neglectus Peck. P. 52
Western Dewberry. . . . . . Rubus ursinus C & S. P. 52
Longanberry . . . . Rubus loganobaccus Bailey. P. 53
Eastern Dewberry. . . . . . Rubus flagellaris Willd. P. 54
Southern Dewberry . . . . . Rubus trivialis Michx. P. 53
Mountain Blackberry . . . . Rubus allegheniensis Porter. P. 54
Early Harvest Blackberry. . Rubus argutus Link. P. 55
Common or European Plum . . Prunus domesticus L. P. 57
Japanese Plum . . . . Prunus salicina Lindl. P. 57
Wild Plum . . . . Prunus americana Marsh. P. 58
Chickasaw Plum. . . . . . . Prunus angustifolia Marsh. P. 58
Sand Plum . . . . Prunus angustifolia watsoni Waugh. P. 58
Wild Goose Plum . . . . . . Prunus hortulana Bailey. P. 59
Common Apricot. . . . . . . Prunus armeniaca L. P. 55
Almond. . . . . Amygdalus communis L. P. 56
Peach . . . . Amygdalus persica L. P. 56
Sour Cherry . . . . Prunus cerasus L. P. 60
Sweet Cherry. . . . . Prunus avium L. P. 59
Medlar. . . . . Mespilus germanica L. P. 60
Quince. . . . . Cydonia oblonga Mill. P. 61
Chinese Quince. . . . . . . Chaenomeles sinensis Koehne. P. 61
Loquat. . . . . Eribotrya japonica Lindl. P. 61
Pear. . . . . Pyrus communis L. P. 62

Chinese or Sand Pear. . . . Pyrus serotina Rehd. P. 62
Apple . . . . Malus malus Britt. P. 62
Siberian Crab . . . . . . Malus baccata Borkh. P. 63
Prairie Crab. . . . . . . Malus ioensis Britt. P. 63
Garland Crab. . . . . . . Malus coronaria Mill. P. 63

PEA FAMILY Leguminosae

Pea . . . . Pisum sativum L. P. 64
Lentil. . . . . Lens esculenta Moench. P. 65
Broad Bean. . . . . Vicia faba L. P. 65
Peanut. . . . . Arachis hypogaea L. P. 64
Kidney Bean . . . . Phaseolus vulgaris L. P. 68
Scarlet Runner. . . . . . Phaseolus coccineus L. P. 68
Sieva Bean. . . . . Phaseolus lunatus L. P. 69
Lima Bean . . . . Phaseolus limensis Maef. P. 69
Asparagus Bean. . . . . . Vigna sesquipedalis Wight. P. 67
Cowpea. . . . . Vigna sinensis Endl. P. 67
Yam Bean. . . . . Pachyrhizus tuberosus Spr. P. 67
Hyacinth Bean . . . . . . Dolichos lablab L. P. 66
Soybean . . . . Glycine max Merr. P. 66
Carob Bean. . . . . Ceratonia siliqua L. P. 63

NASTURTIUM FAMILY Tropaeolaceae

Garden Nasturtium . . . . . Tropaeolum majus L. P. 101
Dwarf Nasturtium. . . . . . Tropaeolum minus L. P. 101
Tuberous-rooted Nasturtium. Tropaeolum tuberosum R & R. P. 101

FLAX FAMILY Linaceae

Flax. . . . . Linum usitatissamum L. P. 145

RUE FAMILY Rutaceae

Citron. . . . . Citrus medica L. P. 70
Lemon . . . . Citrus limonia Osbeck. P. 71
Lime. . . . . Citrus aurantifolia Sw. P. 71
Grapefruit. . . . . Citrus paradisi Sw. P. 72
Shaddock. . . . . Citrus maxima Merr. P. 72
Seville Orange. . . . . . Citrus aurantium L. P. 72
Orange. . . . . Citrus sinensis Osbeck. P. 73
Tangerine . . . . Citrus nobilis deliciosa Sw. P. 73
Satsuma . . . . Citrus nobilis unshiu Sw. P. 73
Calamondin Orange . . . . Citrus mitis Blanco. P. 73
Trifoliate Orange . . . . Poncirus trifoliata Raf. P. 72
Oval Kumquat. . . . . . . Fortunella margarita Sw. P. 70
Meiwa Kumquat . . . . . . Fortunella crassifolia Sw. P. 70
Marumi Kumquat. . . . . . Fortunella japonica Sw. P. 70

SPURGE FAMILY Euphorbiaceae

Castor-Bean . . . . Ricinus communis L. P. 113
Para Rubber-Tree. . . . . Hevea brasiliensis Muell. P. 149

Ceara Rubber. . . . . Manihot glaziovii. P. 149
Tapioca-Plant . . . . Manihot utilissima Pohl. P. 100

CASHEW FAMILY Anacardiaceae

Cashew. . . . . Anacardium occidentale L. P. 119
Mango . . . . Mangifera indica L. P. 138
Pistachio . . . . Pistacia vera L. P. 136

HOLLY FAMILY Aquifoliaceae

Mate'. . . . . Ilex paraguayensis. P. 102

MAPLE FAMILY Aceraceae

Maples. . . . . Acer spp. P. 107

SOAPBERRY FAMILY Sapindaceae

Litchi. . . . . Litchi chinensis Sonn. P. 137
Spanish-Lime. . . . . Melicocca bijuga L. P. 136

BUCKTHORN FAMILY Rhamnaceae

Jujube. . . . . Zizyphus jujuba Mill. P. 139

GRAPE FAMILY Vitaceae

Vinifera Grape. . . . . . . Vitis vinifera L. P. 134
Muscadine Grape . . . . . . Vitis rotundifolia Michx. P. 135
Labruscan Grape . . . . . . Vitis labruscana Bailey. P. 134
River-bank Grape. . . . . . Vitis vulpina L. P. 135

LINDEN FAMILY Tiliaceae

Jute. . . . . Corchorus capsularis L. P. 146
Nalta Jute. . . . . Corchorus olitorius L. P. 146

MALLOW FAMILY Malvaceae

Sea-Island Cotton . . . . . Gossypium barbadense L. P. 142
Upland Cotton . . . . Gossypium hirsutum L. P. 143
Indian Cotton . . . . Gossypium herbaceum L. P. 143
Peruvian Cotton . . . . . . Gossypium peruvianum Cav. P. 143
Tree Cotton . . . . Gossypium arboreum L. P. 143
Okra. . . . . Hibiscus esculentus L. P. 109

BOMBAX FAMILY Bombacaceae

Baobab. . . . . Adansonia digitata L. P. 125

COLA FAMILY Sterculiaceae

Cola. . . . . Cola acuminata S & E. P. 112
Cacao . . . . Theobroma cacao L. P. 112

TEA FAMILY Ternstroemiaceae

Tea . . . . Thea sinensis L. P. 103

PLANTS WE EAT AND WEAR

MANGOSTEEN FAMILY Guttiferae

Mangosteen. . . . . Garcinia mangostana L. P. 128
Mammee-Apple. . . . . . . Mammea americana L. P. 137

PASSION-FLOWER FAMILY Passifloraceae

Wild Passion-Flower . . . . Passiflora incarnata L. P. 122
Granadilla. . . . . Passiflora edulis Sims. P. 122

PAPAW FAMILY Caricaceae

Papaya. . . . . Carica papaya L. P. 128

CACTUS FAMILY Cactaceae

Indian-Fig. . . . . Opuntia ficus-india Mill. P. 121
Tuna. . . . . Opuntia tuna. P. 121

OLEASTER FAMILY Eleagnaceae

Buffalo-Berry . . . . . . Shepherdia argentea Nutt. P. 135

LOOSESTRIFE FAMILY Lythraceae

Henna . . . . Lawsonia inermis L. P. 147

POMEGRANATE FAMILY Punicaceae

Pomegranate . . . . Punica granatum L. P. 129

BRAZIL-NUT FAMILY Lecythidaceae

Brazil Nut. . . . . Bertholletia excelsa H & B. P. 119

MYRTLE FAMILY Myrtaceae

Pitanga . . . . Eugenia uniflora L. P. 127
Australian Bush-Cherry. . . Eugenia myrtifolia Sims. P. 127
Rose-Apple. . . . . Eugenia jambos L. P. 127
Clove-Tree. . . . . Eugenia aromatica Baill. P. 108
Jambolan. . . . . Eugenia jambolana Lam. P. 127
Allspice. . . . . Pimenta officinalis Berg. P. 126
Guava . . . . Psidium guajava L. P. 125
Strawberry Guava. . . . . Psidium cattleianum Sab. P. 126

PARSLEY FAMILY Umbelliferae

Cultivated Carrot . . . . . Daucus carota sativa DC. P. 75
Cumin . . . . Cuminum cyminum L. P. 78
Coriander . . . . Coriandrum sativum L. P. 78
Dill. . . . . Anethum graveolens L. P. 79
Lovage. . . . . Levisticum officinale Koch. P. 80
Parsley . . . . Petroselinum hortense Hoffm. P. 77
Celery. . . . . Apium graveolens dulce DC. P. 76
Celeriac. . . . . Apium graveolens rapaceum DC. P. 76
Anise . . . . Pimpinella anisum L. P. 80
Cultivated Parsnip. . . . . Pastinaca sativa L. P. 75

PLANTS WE EAT AND WEAR

Skirret. . . . . Sium sisarum L. P. 74
Salad Chervil. . . . . . . Anthriscus cerefolium Hoffm. P. 77
Turnip-rooted Chervil. . . . Chaerophyllum bulbosum L. P. 77
Caraway. . . . . Carum carvi L. P. 79

HEATH FAMILY Ericaceae

Wintergreen. . . . . Gaultheria procumbens L. P. 138
High-bush Blueberry. . . . Vaccinium corymbosum L. P. 133
Low Blueberry. . . . . . . Vaccinium pennsylvanicum Lam. P. 133
American Cranberry . . . . Vaccinium macrocarpon Ait. P. 132
European Cranberry . . . . Vaccinium oxycoccus L. P. 132
Hairy Huckleberry. . . . . Vaccinium hirsutum. P. 133
Whortleberry . . . . Vaccinium myrtillus. P. 133
Black Huckleberry. . . . . Gaylussacia baccata Koch. P. 133

SAPODILLA FAMILY Sapotaceae

Canistel . . . . Lucuma nervosa A. DC. P. 124
Gutta-percha Tree. . . . . Palaquium gutta Burck. P. 148
Sapodilla. . . . . Sapota achras Mill. P. 124
Star-Apple . . . . Chrysophyllum cainito L. P. 123

EBONY FAMILY Ebonaceae

Persimmon. . . . . Diospyros virginiana L. P. 123
Japanese Persimmon . . . . Diospyros kaki L.f. P. 123

OLIVE FAMILY Oleaceae

Olive. . . . . Olea europaea L. P. 109

DOGBANE FAMILY Apocynaceae

West African Rubber. . . . Landolphia spp. P. 149
Silk Rubber. . . . . Funtumia elastica. P. 149

MORNING-GLORY FAMILY Convolvulaceae

Sweet-Potato . . . . Ipomoea batatus Lam. P. 99

MINT FAMILY Labiate

Sage . . . . Salvia officinalis L. P. 81
Thyme. . . . . Thymus vulgaris L. P. 83
Mother of Thyme. . . . . . Thymus serphyllum L. P. 83
Catnip . . . . Nepeta cataria L. P. 83
Peppermint . . . . Mentha piperita L. P. 84
Spearmint. . . . . Mentha spicata L. P. 84
Pennyroyal . . . . Mentha pulequim L. P. 84
Hyssop . . . . Hyssopus officinalis L. P. 82
Summer Savory. . . . . . . Satureja hortensis L. P. 82
Winter Savory. . . . . . . Satureja montana L. P. 82

PLANTS WE EAT AND WEAR

NIGHTSHADE FAMILY Solanaceae

Potato. . . . . Solanum tuberosum L. P. 85
Wonderberry . . . . Solanum nigrum L. P. 86
Common Eggplant . . . . . Solanum melongena esculenta Nees. P. 86
Scarlet Eggplant. . . . . Solanum integrifolium Poir. P. 86
Tomato. . . . . Lycopersicon esculentum commune Bailey. P.87
Tree-Tomato . . . . Cyphomandra betacea Sendt. P. 87
Strawberry-Tomato . . . . Physalis pubescens L. P. 89
Tomatiilo . . . . Physalis ixocarpa Brot. P. 89
Cape-Gooseberry . . . . . Physalis peruviana L. P. 90
Tobacco. . . . . Nicotiana tabacum L. P. 85
Sweet or Bell Pepper. . . Capsicum frutescens grossum Bailey. P. 88
Red Pepper. . . . . Capsicum frutescens L. P. 88

MADDER FAMILY Rubiaceae

Madder. . . . . Rubia tinctorum L. P. 146
Coffee. . . . . Coffea arabica L. P. 111

HONEYSUCKLE FAMILY Caprifoliaceae

Elderberry. . . . . Sambucus canadensis L. P. 130
High Cranberry. . . . . . Viburnum trilobum L. P. 132
Black-Haw . . . . Viburnum prunifolium L. P. 132

GOURD FAMILY Cucurbitaceae

Field and Other Pumpkins. . Curcurbita pepo L. P. 91
Cheese, Cushaw and other
   Pumpkins . . . . Cucurbita moschata Duch. P. 91
Squashes. . . . . Cucurbita maxima Duch. P. 92
Chinese Preserving Melon. . Benincasa hispida Cogn. P. 92
Watermelon. . . . . Citrullus vulgaris Schrad. P. 93
Bur Gherkin . . . . Cucumis anguria L. P. 94
Cucumber. . . . . Cucumis sativus L. P. 94
Muskmelon . . . . Cucumis melo L. P. 93
Chayote . . . . Sechium edule Sw. P. 90

COMPOSITE FAMILY Compositae

Chicory . . . . Cicorium intybus L. P. 97
Endive. . . . . Cicorium endivia L. P. 96
Dandelion . . . . Taraxacum officinale Weber. P. 98
Salsify . . . . Tragopogon porrifolius L. P. 96
Lettuce . . . . Lactuca sativa L. P. 95
Common Sunflower. . . . . Helianthus annuus L. P. 97
Jerusalem Artichoke . . . Helianthus tuberosus L. P. 97
Globe Artichoke . . . . . Cynara scolymus L. P. 98
Cardoon . . . . Cynara cardunculus L. P. 98

INDEX

It will be noted that the uncapitalized items represent the species names of the plants described in this book.

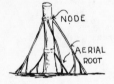

avellana 114
Avena 31
avium 59
Avocado 138,153
Axil. The point on a stem just above the base of a leaf. (Fig. 279)

Fig. 279

B

baccata 63,133
Bacteria 16
Bailey 6
Banana 35,151
Banana Squash 92
Banyan 140
Baobab 125,156
barbadense 142
Barbarea 49
Barley 31,151
batatas 39,99
Beech 118,152
Beet 101,153
Belleville Spinach 104
Bell Pepper 88,159
Benicasa 92
Berry 10
Bertholletia 119
Beta 101
betacea 87
Biennial. A plant that grows vegetatively one year and flowers, matures seed and dies the second year.
Big Shellbark Hickory 115
bijuga 136
Billberry 133
Bitter-Cress 48,154
Bitternut 115
Black Apricot 55
Blackberry 51
Blackcap Raspberry 51,154
Black Currant 131,154
Black-Haw 132,159
Black Huckleberry 133,158
Black Mulberry 140,152
Black Mustard 45,153
Black Walnut 117,152
Bletting. An over ripening process. 60

Bloom. A whitish powder sometimes covering fruit.
Blueberry 133
Blue Elder 130
Boehmeria 145
Boletus 19
Boll. Seed pod of Cotton plant. (Fig. 280)

Fig. 280

Bonavist 66
Borecole 49,153
botrytis 44
Bract. A modified leaf having a flower in its axil. (Fig. 281)

Fig. 281

brasiliensis 149
Brassica 41
Brazil Nut 119,157
Bread-Fruit 139,152
Broad Bean 65,155
Broccoli 44
Broom Corn 28,150
Broom-Corn Millet 29,151
Brussels Sprouts 47,153
Bryophyta 6
Buckwheat 114,152
Buffalo Berry 135,157
Buffalo Currant 131,154
Bulb. A bud with fleshy scales for reproduction. (Fig. 282)

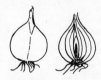

Fig. 282

bulbifera 39
Bulbil. Small bulbs often growing as aerial structures. (Fig. 283)

161

Fig. 283

bulbosum 77
Bur Gherkin 94,159
Bush Lima 69
Buttercup Squash 92
Butternut 117,152

C

Cabbage 46,153
Cacao 112,156
cafforum 27
cainito 123
Calamondin Orange 73,155
Calcium 7
Calla Lily 33
Calyx. The outer set of floral parts; the sepals taken collectively, 12. (Fig. 284)

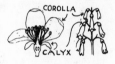

Fig. 284

campestris 19
Camphor Tree 108
canadensis 130
Cananga 147
Cane sugar 8
Canistel 124,158
Cannabis 144
Cantaloupe 93
cantalupensis 93
Cape-Gooseberry 90,159
Caper-Bud 99,153
capita 95
capitata 46
Capparis 99
Capsicum 88
capsularis 146
Capsule. A dry dehiscent fruit with two or more carpels. (Fig. 285)
Caraway 79,158
Carbon 7

Fig. 285

Carbon dioxide 7
Cardamine 48
Cardoon 98,159
cardunçulus 98
Carica 128
carica 140
Carob 63,155
carota 75
Carpegonium 17
Carpel. One section of a
  pistil.
Carpelate flower. Same as
  pistillate flower.
Carragheen 17
Carrot 75
cartilagineum 17
Carum 79
carvi 79
Carya 115
Cashew 119,156
Cassava 100
cassia 108
Cassia-Bark-Tree 108,153
Castanea 118,119
Castilla 149
Castor Bean 11,113,155
Castor-Oil-Plant 113
cataria 83
cathayensis 116
Catmint 83
Catnip 83,158
cattleianum 126
Cauliflower 44,153
caulorapa 41
Cayenne Pepper 88
Ceara Rubber 149,156
Celeriac 76,157
Celery 76,157
Celery Cabbage 46
Celestial Pepper 88
Cell. Individual struc-
  tural unit of a plant. 16
  (Fig. 286)

Figure 286. Plant
cells in a stem.

Century Plant 34

cepa 38
cerasus 60
Ceratonia 63
cereale 32
cerefolium 77
Ceriman 15,33,151
cerivisiae 16
Cetaria 18
Cetrullus 93
Ceylon Moss 17
Chaenomeles 61
Chaerophyllum 77
Chard 106
Chayote 90,159
Cheese Pumpkin 91,159
cherimola 141
Cherimoya 141,153
Cherry-Pepper 88
Chestnut 118,152
Chickasaw Plum 58,154
Chickle 124
Chicory 97,159
chiloensis 50
chinensis 20,46,137
Chinese Cabbage 46,153
Chinese Fan-Palm 20,151
Chinese Lantern Plant 90
Chinese Moss 17
Chinese Mustard 45
Chinese Pear 62,155
Chinese Preserving Melon
  92,159
Chinese Quince 61,154
Chinese Walnut 116,152
Chinese Watermelon 92
Chinese Yam 39,151
Chinquipin 118
chito 93
Chive 37,151
Chlorophyll. The green
  coloring matter in plants.
  17
Chondrus 17
Christophine 90
Chrysophyllum 123
Ciboule 39
Cichorium 96
cicla 106
cinerea 117
Cinnamon Tree 108,153
Cinnamomum 108
citroides 93
Citron 70,93,155
Citrus 70
Cive 37
Climbing Ylang-Ylang 147,
  153
Clove Tree 108,157
coccineus 68

Coconut 21 151
Cocos 21
Coffea 111
Coffee 111,159
Coir 21
Coix 26
Cola 112,156
Collards 49
Collective fruit. Formed
  from several flowers.
  (Fig. 287)

Fig. 287

Colocasia 33
Common Apricot 55,154
Common Currant 131,154
Common Eggplant 86,159
Common Fig 140,152
Common Ginger 40,151
Common Morel 18,150
Common Mushroom 19,150
Common Onion 38,151
Common Plum 57,154
Common Sunflower 97,159
Common Vanilla 36,152
commune 87
communis 56,62,113,139
Complete flower. Having
  sepals, petals, stamens
  and pistil. 12
  (Fig. 288)

Fig. 288

comosus 35
Compound leaf. With the
  blade cut into two or
  more leaflets.
  (Fig. 289)

Fig. 289

162

Fig. 299

Fig. 300

Fig. 301

Fig. 302

165

Fig. 303

Fig. 304

Orach 105,153
Orange 73,155
Orchid 36
Oryza 30
Oval Kumquat 70,155
Ovary. The enlarged part
of the pistil. 13
(Fig. 305)
ovata 115
ovifera 91
Ovule. Part in ovary
which becomes a seed. 13
(Fig. 305)

Figure 305

oxycoccus 132
Oxygen 7
Oyster Mushroom 19
Oyster Plant 96

P

Pachyrhizus 67
Pakchoi 46,154
Palaquium 148
Palm 20,21
Palmaceae 20
Palma Christi 113
Palmate leaf. With all the
leaflets radiating from
one point of attachment.
(Fig. 306)

Figure 306

Palmetto 20
Panicle. A flower cluster
in which some of the
branches branch again.
(Fig. 307)
Panicum 29
Papaver 106
Papaya 128,157
parachinensis 46

Figure 307

paradisi 72
paradisica 35
paraguayensis 102
Para Rubber 149,155
Parsley 77,157
Parsnip 75
Passiflora 122
Passion Flower 122
Pastinaca 75
patientia 105
Pea 64,155
Peach 56,154
Peanut 64,155
Pear 62,154
Pearl Millet 29,151
Pecan 115,152
Pedicel. Flower or fruit
stem. 12
pekinensis 46
Pennisetum 29
pennsylvanicum 133
Pennyroyal 84,158
Pepo. A fruit of melon
or cucumber type.
pepo 91
Pepper 111,152
Peppermint 84,158
Perfect flower. Having
both male and female
parts; stamens and
pistil. 14
Perfection Pepper 88
Perry 62
Persea 138
persica 56
Persimmon 123,158
peruviana 90,143
Peruvian Cotton 143,156
Petal. One leaf of the
corolla.
Petiole. A leaf stem.
(Fig. 308)

Figure 308

Petroselinum 77

Pe-tsai 46,153
Phaseolus 68
Phenomenal 53
Phoenix 21
Phormium 145
Phosphorous 7
Photosynthesis 8
Physalis 89
Pie Pumpkin 91
Pignut 115
Pimenta 126
Pimento 126
Pimpinella 80
Pina cloth 35
Pineapple 35,151
Pinnate leaf. With leaf-
lets scattered along an
axis. (Fig. 309)

Figure 309

Piper 111
piperita 84
Pistachio 136,156
Pistacia 136
Pistil. Female organ at
middle of flower. 13
(Fig. 310)

Figure 310

Pistillate flower. Having
pistil but no stamens; a
female flower. (Fig. 310)
Pisum 64
Pitanga 127,157
planifolia 36
Plant names 14
Plant Poisons 11
Plant proteins 8
Pod Corn 23,150
Poison-Hemlock 74
Pollination. The transfer
of pollen from the anther
to the stigma. 14
Pome 10
Pomegranate 129,157
Poncirus 72
Pop Corn 23,150

Q

R

Figure 311

Figure 312

Figure 313

Figure 314

S

Figure 315

Sessile. Leaf or flower
having no stem.
(Fig. 316)

Figure 316

Setaria 30
Seville Orange 72,155
Shaddock 72,155
Shagbark Hickory 115,152
Shaggy Mane 19
Shallot 38,151
Shepherdia 135
Siberian Crab 63,155
sieboldiana 116
Sieva Bean 69,155
siliqua 63
Silique. A two-valved
fruit with seeds at-
tached in two rows.
(Fig. 317)

Figure 317

Silk Rubber 149,158
sinensis 61,67,73,103
Sisal 34
sisarum 74
Sium 74
Skirret 74,158
Snake Eggplant 86
Snake Melon 93
Snowball 132
Soft Corn 24,150
Solanum 85
somniferum 106
Sorghum 27
Sour Cherry 60,154
Sour Gourd 125
Sour Orange 72
Soursop 141,153
South American Apricot 137
Southern Dewberry 53,154

Soybean 66,155
Spadix. A flower spike
with a fleshy axis.
(Fig. 318)

Figure 318

Spanish-Lime 136,156
Spathe. A bract surround-
ing a spadix as in the
Calla Lily. (Fig. 318)
Spearmint 84,158
spectabilis 51
Spermatophyta 5
spicata 84
Spike. Sessile flowers
arranged along an axis.
(Fig. 319)

Figure 319

Spikelet. Small spike, as
in the grasses.
Spinach 105,153
Spinach Dock 105,153
Spinacia 105
spinosa 99
Sponge Mushroom 18
Spores 5
Spring Onion 39
Sprouting Broccoli 44,153
squamosa 141
Squashes 92,159
Stamen. Part of flower
producing the pollen. 13
(Fig. 320)

Figure 320

Staminate flower. Having
stamens but no pistil; a
male flower. (Fig. 320)
Star-Apple 123,158
Starch 8
Stem-turnip 41

Sterile. Flowers that
cannot produce pollen or
seed.
Stigma. Upper part of
pistil which receives
the pollen. 13 (Fig. 321)

Figure 321

St. Johns-Bread 63
Strawberry 50,154
Strawberry Guava 125,157
Strawberry-Tomato 89,159
String Bean 68
Stringless Bean 68
Sturtevant 6
Style. A short or longer
stem often connecting
the stigma and ovary. 13
(Fig. 321)
Suckers. Young plants
sprouting from the base
of a parent plant as in
Corn. (Fig. 322)

Figure 322

Sugar-Apple 141,153
Sugar Beet 101
Sugar-Cane 26,150
Sulphur 7
Summer Radish 42
Summer Savory 82,158
Summer Scallop Squash 91
Sunberry 86
Surinam-cherry 127
Swamp Blueberry 133
Swedes 43
Swede Turnip 43
Sweet Cherry 59,154
Sweet Corn 24,150
Sweet Elder 130
Sweet Orange 73
Sweet Pepper 88,159
Sweet-Potato 99,158
Sweet Sorghum 27,150
Swiss Chard 106,153
sylvatica 118
sylvestris 75

A CATALOGUE OF SELECTED DOVER BOOKS
IN ALL FIELDS OF INTEREST

AMERICA'S OLD MASTERS, James T. Flexner. Four men emerged unexpectedly from provincial 18th century America to leadership in European art: Benjamin West, J. S. Copley, C. R. Peale, Gilbert Stuart. Brilliant coverage of lives and contributions. Revised, 1967 edition. 69 plates. 365pp. of text.

21806-6 Paperbound $3.00

FIRST FLOWERS OF OUR WILDERNESS: AMERICAN PAINTING, THE COLONIAL PERIOD, James T. Flexner. Painters, and regional painting traditions from earliest Colonial times up to the emergence of Copley, West and Peale Sr., Foster, Gustavus Hesselius, Feke, John Smibert and many anonymous painters in the primitive manner. Engaging presentation, with 162 illustrations. xxii + 368pp.

22180-6 Paperbound $3.50

THE LIGHT OF DISTANT SKIES: AMERICAN PAINTING, 1760-1835, James T. Flexner. The great generation of early American painters goes to Europe to learn and to teach: West, Copley, Gilbert Stuart and others. Allston, Trumbull, Morse; also contemporary American painters—primitives, derivatives, academics—who remained in America. 102 illustrations. xiii + 306pp.

22179-2 Paperbound $3.00

A HISTORY OF THE RISE AND PROGRESS OF THE ARTS OF DESIGN IN THE UNITED STATES, William Dunlap. Much the richest mine of information on early American painters, sculptors, architects, engravers, miniaturists, etc. The only source of information for scores of artists, the major primary source for many others. Unabridged reprint of rare original 1834 edition, with new introduction by James T. Flexner, and 394 new illustrations. Edited by Rita Weiss. 6⅝ x 9⅝.

21695-0, 21696-9, 21697-7 Three volumes, Paperbound $13.50

EPOCHS OF CHINESE AND JAPANESE ART, Ernest F. Fenollosa. From primitive Chinese art to the 20th century, thorough history, explanation of every important art period and form, including Japanese woodcuts; main stress on China and Japan, but Tibet, Korea also included. Still unexcelled for its detailed, rich coverage of cultural background, aesthetic elements, diffusion studies, particularly of the historical period. 2nd, 1913 edition. 242 illustrations. lii + 439pp. of text.

20364-6, 20365-4 Two volumes, Paperbound $6.00

THE GENTLE ART OF MAKING ENEMIES, James A. M. Whistler. Greatest wit of his day deflates Oscar Wilde, Ruskin, Swinburne; strikes back at inane critics, exhibitions, art journalism; aesthetics of impressionist revolution in most striking form. Highly readable classic by great painter. Reproduction of edition designed by Whistler. Introduction by Alfred Werner. xxxvi + 334pp.

21875-9 Paperbound $2.50

How to Know the Wild Flowers, Mrs. William Starr Dana. This is the classical book of American wildflowers (of the Eastern and Central United States), used by hundreds of thousands. Covers over 500 species, arranged in extremely easy to use color and season groups. Full descriptions, much plant lore. This Dover edition is the fullest ever compiled, with tables of nomenclature changes. 174 full-page plates by M. Satterlee. xii + 418pp. 20332-8 Paperbound $2.75

Our Plant Friends and Foes, William Atherton DuPuy. History, economic importance, essential botanical information and peculiarities of 25 common forms of plant life are provided in this book in an entertaining and charming style. Covers food plants (potatoes, apples, beans, wheat, almonds, bananas, etc.), flowers (lily, tulip, etc.), trees (pine, oak, elm, etc.), weeds, poisonous mushrooms and vines, gourds, citrus fruits, cotton, the cactus family, and much more. 108 illustrations. xiv + 290pp. 22272-1 Paperbound $2.50

How to Know the Ferns, Frances T. Parsons. Classic survey of Eastern and Central ferns, arranged according to clear, simple identification key. Excellent introduction to greatly neglected nature area. 57 illustrations and 42 plates. xvi + 215pp. 20740-4 Paperbound $2.00

Manual of the Trees of North America, Charles S. Sargent. America's foremost dendrologist provides the definitive coverage of North American trees and tree-like shrubs. 717 species fully described and illustrated: exact distribution, down to township; full botanical description; economic importance; description of subspecies and races; habitat, growth data; similar material. Necessary to every serious student of tree-life. Nomenclature revised to present. Over 100 locating keys. 783 illustrations. lii + 934pp. 20277-1, 20278-X Two volumes, Paperbound $6.00

Our Northern Shrubs, Harriet L. Keeler. Fine non-technical reference work identifying more than 225 important shrubs of Eastern and Central United States and Canada. Full text covering botanical description, habitat, plant lore, is paralleled with 205 full-page photographs of flowering or fruiting plants. Nomenclature revised by Edward G. Voss. One of few works concerned with shrubs. 205 plates, 35 drawings. xxviii + 521pp. 21989-5 Paperbound $3.75

The Mushroom Handbook, Louis C. C. Krieger. Still the best popular handbook: full descriptions of 259 species, cross references to another 200. Extremely thorough text enables you to identify, know all about any mushroom you are likely to meet in eastern and central U. S. A.: habitat, luminescence, poisonous qualities, use, folklore, etc. 32 color plates show over 50 mushrooms, also 126 other illustrations. Finding keys. vii + 560pp. 21861-9 Paperbound $3.95

Handbook of Birds of Eastern North America, Frank M. Chapman. Still much the best single-volume guide to the birds of Eastern and Central United States. Very full coverage of 675 species, with descriptions, life habits, distribution, similar data. All descriptions keyed to two-page color chart. With this single volume the average birdwatcher needs no other books. 1931 revised edition. 195 illustrations. xxxvi + 581pp. 21489-3 Paperbound $5.00

ALPHABETS AND ORNAMENTS, Ernst Lehner. Well-known pictorial source for decorative alphabets, script examples, cartouches, frames, decorative title pages, calligraphic initials, borders, similar material. 14th to 19th century, mostly European. Useful in almost any graphic arts designing, varied styles. 750 illustrations. 256pp. 7 x 10.   21905-4 Paperbound $4.00

PAINTING: A CREATIVE APPROACH, Norman Colquhoun. For the beginner simple guide provides an instructive approach to painting: major stumbling blocks for beginner; overcoming them, technical points; paints and pigments; oil painting; watercolor and other media and color. New section on "plastic" paints. Glossary. Formerly *Paint Your Own Pictures*. 221pp.   22000-1 Paperbound $1.75

THE ENJOYMENT AND USE OF COLOR, Walter Sargent. Explanation of the relations between colors themselves and between colors in nature and art, including hundreds of little-known facts about color values, intensities, effects of high and low illumination, complementary colors. Many practical hints for painters, references to great masters. 7 color plates, 29 illustrations. x + 274pp.
                                                               20944-X Paperbound $2.75

THE NOTEBOOKS OF LEONARDO DA VINCI, compiled and edited by Jean Paul Richter. 1566 extracts from original manuscripts reveal the full range of Leonardo's versatile genius: all his writings on painting, sculpture, architecture, anatomy, astronomy, geography, topography, physiology, mining, music, etc., in both Italian and English, with 186 plates of manuscript pages and more than 500 additional drawings. Includes studies for the Last Supper, the lost Sforza monument, and other works. Total of xlvii + 866pp. 7⅞ x 10¾.
                                  22572-0, 22573-9 Two volumes, Paperbound $10.00

MONTGOMERY WARD CATALOGUE OF 1895. Tea gowns, yards of flannel and pillow-case lace, stereoscopes, books of gospel hymns, the New Improved Singer Sewing Machine, side saddles, milk skimmers, straight-edged razors, high-button shoes, spittoons, and on and on . . . listing some 25,000 items, practically all illustrated. Essential to the shoppers of the 1890's, it is our truest record of the spirit of the period. Unaltered reprint of Issue No. 57, Spring and Summer 1895. Introduction by Boris Emmet. Innumerable illustrations. xiii + 624pp. 8½ x 11⅝.
                                                               22377-9 Paperbound $6.95

THE CRYSTAL PALACE EXHIBITION ILLUSTRATED CATALOGUE (LONDON, 1851). One of the wonders of the modern world—the Crystal Palace Exhibition in which all the nations of the civilized world exhibited their achievements in the arts and sciences—presented in an equally important illustrated catalogue. More than 1700 items pictured with accompanying text—ceramics, textiles, cast-iron work, carpets, pianos, sleds, razors, wall-papers, billiard tables, beehives, silverware and hundreds of other artifacts—represent the focal point of Victorian culture in the Western World. Probably the largest collection of Victorian decorative art ever assembled— indispensable for antiquarians and designers. Unabridged republication of the Art-Journal Catalogue of the Great Exhibition of 1851, with all terminal essays. New introduction by John Gloag, F.S.A. xxxiv + 426pp. 9 x 12.
                                                               22503-8 Paperbound $4.50

AMERICAN FOOD AND GAME FISHES, David S. Jordan and Barton W. Evermann. Definitive source of information, detailed and accurate enough to enable the sportsman and nature lover to identify conclusively some 1,000 species and sub-species of North American fish, sought for food or sport. Coverage of range, physiology, habits, life history, food value. Best methods of capture, interest to the angler, advice on bait, fly-fishing, etc. 338 drawings and photographs. l + 574pp. 6⅝ x 9⅜.
22383-1 Paperbound $4.50

THE FROG BOOK, Mary C. Dickerson. Complete with extensive finding keys, over 300 photographs, and an introduction to the general biology of frogs and toads, this is the classic non-technical study of Northeastern and Central species. 58 species; 290 photographs and 16 color plates. xvii + 253pp.
21973-9 Paperbound $4.00

THE MOTH BOOK: A GUIDE TO THE MOTHS OF NORTH AMERICA, William J. Holland. Classical study, eagerly sought after and used for the past 60 years. Clear identification manual to more than 2,000 different moths, largest manual in existence. General information about moths, capturing, mounting, classifying, etc., followed by species by species descriptions. 263 illustrations plus 48 color plates show almost every species, full size. 1968 edition, preface, nomenclature changes by A. E. Brower. xxiv + 479pp. of text. 6½ x 9¼.
21948-8 Paperbound $5.00

THE SEA-BEACH AT EBB-TIDE, Augusta Foote Arnold. Interested amateur can identify hundreds of marine plants and animals on coasts of North America; marine algae; seaweeds; squids; hermit crabs; horse shoe crabs; shrimps; corals; sea anemones; etc. Species descriptions cover: structure; food; reproductive cycle; size; shape; color; habitat; etc. Over 600 drawings. 85 plates. xii + 490pp.
21949-6 Paperbound $3.50

COMMON BIRD SONGS, Donald J. Borror. 33⅓ 12-inch record presents songs of 60 important birds of the eastern United States. A thorough, serious record which provides several examples for each bird, showing different types of song, individual variations, etc. Inestimable identification aid for birdwatcher. 32-page booklet gives text about birds and songs, with illustration for each bird.
21829-5 Record, book, album. Monaural. $2.75

FADS AND FALLACIES IN THE NAME OF SCIENCE, Martin Gardner. Fair, witty appraisal of cranks and quacks of science: Atlantis, Lemuria, hollow earth, flat earth, Velikovsky, orgone energy, Dianetics, flying saucers, Bridey Murphy, food fads, medical fads, perpetual motion, etc. Formerly "In the Name of Science." x + 363pp.
20394-8 Paperbound $2.00

HOAXES, Curtis D. MacDougall. Exhaustive, unbelievably rich account of great hoaxes: Locke's moon hoax, Shakespearean forgeries, sea serpents, Loch Ness monster, Cardiff giant, John Wilkes Booth's mummy, Disumbrationist school of art, dozens more; also journalism, psychology of hoaxing. 54 illustrations. xi + 338pp.
20465-0 Paperbound $2.75

THE PRINCIPLES OF PSYCHOLOGY, William James. The famous long course, complete and unabridged. Stream of thought, time perception, memory, experimental methods—these are only some of the concerns of a work that was years ahead of its time and still valid, interesting, useful. 94 figures. Total of xviii + 1391pp.
20381-6, 20382-4 Two volumes, Paperbound $8.00

THE STRANGE STORY OF THE QUANTUM, Banesh Hoffmann. Non-mathematical but thorough explanation of work of Planck, Einstein, Bohr, Pauli, de Broglie, Schrödinger, Heisenberg, Dirac, Feynman, etc. No technical background needed. "Of books attempting such an account, this is the best," Henry Margenau, Yale. 40-page "Postscript 1959." xii + 285pp. 20518-5 Paperbound $2.00

THE RISE OF THE NEW PHYSICS, A. d'Abro. Most thorough explanation in print of central core of mathematical physics, both classical and modern; from Newton to Dirac and Heisenberg. Both history and exposition; philosophy of science, causality, explanations of higher mathematics, analytical mechanics, electromagnetism, thermodynamics, phase rule, special and general relativity, matrices. No higher mathematics needed to follow exposition, though treatment is elementary to intermediate in level. Recommended to serious student who wishes verbal understanding. 97 illustrations. xvii + 982pp. 20003-5, 20004-3 Two volumes, Paperbound $6.00

GREAT IDEAS OF OPERATIONS RESEARCH, Jagjit Singh. Easily followed non-technical explanation of mathematical tools, aims, results: statistics, linear programming, game theory, queueing theory, Monte Carlo simulation, etc. Uses only elementary mathematics. Many case studies, several analyzed in detail. Clarity, breadth make this excellent for specialist in another field who wishes background. 41 figures. x + 228pp. 21886-4 Paperbound $2.50

GREAT IDEAS OF MODERN MATHEMATICS: THEIR NATURE AND USE, Jagjit Singh. Internationally famous expositor, winner of Unesco's Kalinga Award for science popularization explains verbally such topics as differential equations, matrices, groups, sets, transformations, mathematical logic and other important modern mathematics, as well as use in physics, astrophysics, and similar fields. Superb exposition for layman, scientist in other areas. viii + 312pp.
20587-8 Paperbound $2.50

GREAT IDEAS IN INFORMATION THEORY, LANGUAGE AND CYBERNETICS, Jagjit Singh. The analog and digital computers, how they work, how they are like and unlike the human brain, the men who developed them, their future applications, computer terminology. An essential book for today, even for readers with little math. Some mathematical demonstrations included for more advanced readers. 118 figures. Tables. ix + 338pp. 21694-2 Paperbound $2.50

CHANCE, LUCK AND STATISTICS, Horace C. Levinson. Non-mathematical presentation of fundamentals of probability theory and science of statistics and their applications. Games of chance, betting odds, misuse of statistics, normal and skew distributions, birth rates, stock speculation, insurance. Enlarged edition. Formerly "The Science of Chance." xiii + 357pp. 21007-3 Paperbound $2.50

PLANETS, STARS AND GALAXIES: DESCRIPTIVE ASTRONOMY FOR BEGINNERS, A. E. Fanning. Comprehensive introductory survey of astronomy: the sun, solar system, stars, galaxies, universe, cosmology; up-to-date, including quasars, radio stars, etc. Preface by Prof. Donald Menzel. 24pp. of photographs. 189pp. 5¼ x 8¼.
21680-2 Paperbound $1.75

TEACH YOURSELF CALCULUS, P. Abbott. With a good background in algebra and trig, you can teach yourself calculus with this book. Simple, straightforward introduction to functions of all kinds, integration, differentiation, series, etc. "Students who are beginning to study calculus method will derive great help from this book." Faraday House Journal. 308pp. 20683-1 Clothbound $2.50

TEACH YOURSELF TRIGONOMETRY, P. Abbott. Geometrical foundations, indices and logarithms, ratios, angles, circular measure, etc. are presented in this sound, easy-to-use text. Excellent for the beginner or as a brush up, this text carries the student through the solution of triangles. 204pp. 20682-3 Clothbound $2.50

BASIC MACHINES AND HOW THEY WORK, U. S. Bureau of Naval Personnel. Originally used in U.S. Naval training schools, this book clearly explains the operation of a progression of machines, from the simplest—lever, wheel and axle, inclined plane, wedge, screw—to the most complex—typewriter, internal combustion engine, computer mechanism. Utilizing an approach that requires only an elementary understanding of mathematics, these explanations build logically upon each other and are assisted by over 200 drawings and diagrams. Perfect as a technical school manual or as a self-teaching aid to the layman. 204 figures. Preface. Index. vii + 161pp. 6½ x 9¼. 21709-4 Paperbound $2.50

THE FRIENDLY STARS, Martha Evans Martin. Classic has taught naked-eye observation of stars, planets to hundreds of thousands, still not surpassed for charm, lucidity, adequacy. Completely updated by Professor Donald H. Menzel, Harvard Observatory. 25 illustrations. 16 x 30 chart. x + 147pp. 21099-5 Paperbound $1.50

MUSIC OF THE SPHERES: THE MATERIAL UNIVERSE FROM ATOM TO QUASAR, SIMPLY EXPLAINED, Guy Murchie. Extremely broad, brilliantly written popular account begins with the solar system and reaches to dividing line between matter and nonmatter; latest understandings presented with exceptional clarity. Volume One: Planets, stars, galaxies, cosmology, geology, celestial mechanics, latest astronomical discoveries; Volume Two: Matter, atoms, waves, radiation, relativity, chemical action, heat, nuclear energy, quantum theory, music, light, color, probability, antimatter, antigravity, and similar topics. 319 figures. 1967 (second) edition. Total of xx + 644pp. 21809-0, 21810-4 Two volumes, Paperbound $5.50

OLD-TIME SCHOOLS AND SCHOOL BOOKS, Clifton Johnson. Illustrations and rhymes from early primers, abundant quotations from early textbooks, many anecdotes of school life enliven this study of elementary schools from Puritans to middle 19th century. Introduction by Carl Withers. 234 illustrations. xxxiii + 381pp.
21031-6 Paperbound $3.50

THE PHILOSOPHY OF THE UPANISHADS, Paul Deussen. Clear, detailed statement of upanishadic system of thought, generally considered among best available. History of these works, full exposition of system emergent from them, parallel concepts in the West. Translated by A. S. Geden. xiv + 429pp.

21616-0 Paperbound $3.50

LANGUAGE, TRUTH AND LOGIC, Alfred J. Ayer. Famous, remarkably clear introduction to the Vienna and Cambridge schools of Logical Positivism; function of philosophy, elimination of metaphysical thought, nature of analysis, similar topics. "Wish I had written it myself," Bertrand Russell. 2nd, 1946 edition. 160pp.

20010-8 Paperbound $1.50

THE GUIDE FOR THE PERPLEXED, Moses Maimonides. Great classic of medieval Judaism, major attempt to reconcile revealed religion (Pentateuch, commentaries) and Aristotelian philosophy. Enormously important in all Western thought. Unabridged Friedländer translation. 50-page introduction. lix + 414pp.

(USO) 20351-4 Paperbound $3.50

OCCULT AND SUPERNATURAL PHENOMENA, D. H. Rawcliffe. Full, serious study of the most persistent delusions of mankind: crystal gazing, mediumistic trance, stigmata, lycanthropy, fire walking, dowsing, telepathy, ghosts, ESP, etc., and their relation to common forms of abnormal psychology. Formerly *Illusions and Delusions of the Supernatural and the Occult.* iii + 551pp.   20503-7 Paperbound $3.50

THE EGYPTIAN BOOK OF THE DEAD: THE PAPYRUS OF ANI, E. A. Wallis Budge. Full hieroglyphic text, interlinear transliteration of sounds, word for word translation, then smooth, connected translation; Theban recension. Basic work in Ancient Egyptian civilization; now even more significant than ever for historical importance, dilation of consciousness, etc. clvi + 377pp. 6½ x 9¼.

21866-X Paperbound $3.95

PSYCHOLOGY OF MUSIC, Carl E. Seashore. Basic, thorough survey of everything known about psychology of music up to 1940's; essential reading for psychologists, musicologists. Physical acoustics; auditory apparatus; relationship of physical sound to perceived sound; role of the mind in sorting, altering, suppressing, creating sound sensations; musical learning, testing for ability, absolute pitch, other topics. Records of Caruso, Menuhin analyzed. 88 figures. xix + 408pp.

21851-1 Paperbound $3.50

THE I CHING (THE BOOK OF CHANGES), translated by James Legge. Complete translated text plus appendices by Confucius, of perhaps the most penetrating divination book ever compiled. Indispensable to all study of early Oriental civilizations. 3 plates. xxiii + 448pp.   21062-6 Paperbound $3.00

THE UPANISHADS, translated by Max Müller. Twelve classical upanishads: Chandogya, Kena, Aitareya, Kaushitaki, Isa, Katha, Mundaka, Taittiriyaka, Brhadaranyaka, Svetasvatara, Prasna, Maitriyana. 160-page introduction, analysis by Prof. Müller. Total of 670pp. 20992-X, 20993-8 Two volumes, Paperbound $6.50

JIM WHITEWOLF: THE LIFE OF A KIOWA APACHE INDIAN, Charles S. Brant, editor. Spans transition between native life and acculturation period, 1880 on. Kiowa culture, personal life pattern, religion and the supernatural, the Ghost Dance, breakdown in the White Man's world, similar material. 1 map. xii + 144pp.

22015-X Paperbound $1.75

THE NATIVE TRIBES OF CENTRAL AUSTRALIA, Baldwin Spencer and F. J. Gillen. Basic book in anthropology, devoted to full coverage of the Arunta and Warramunga tribes; the source for knowledge about kinship systems, material and social culture, religion, etc. Still unsurpassed. 121 photographs, 89 drawings. xviii + 669pp.

21775-2 Paperbound $5.00

MALAY MAGIC, Walter W. Skeat. Classic (1900); still the definitive work on the folklore and popular religion of the Malay peninsula. Describes marriage rites, birth spirits and ceremonies, medicine, dances, games, war and weapons, etc. Extensive quotes from original sources, many magic charms translated into English. 35 illustrations. Preface by Charles Otto Blagden. xxiv + 685pp.

21760-4 Paperbound $4.00

HEAVENS ON EARTH: UTOPIAN COMMUNITIES IN AMERICA, 1680-1880, Mark Holloway. The finest nontechnical account of American utopias, from the early Woman in the Wilderness, Ephrata, Rappites to the enormous mid 19th-century efflorescence; Shakers, New Harmony, Equity Stores, Fourier's Phalanxes, Oneida, Amana, Fruitlands, etc. "Entertaining and very instructive." *Times Literary Supplement*. 15 illustrations. 246pp.

21593-8 Paperbound $2.00

LONDON LABOUR AND THE LONDON POOR, Henry Mayhew. Earliest (c. 1850) sociological study in English, describing myriad subcultures of London poor. Particularly remarkable for the thousands of pages of direct testimony taken from the lips of London prostitutes, thieves, beggars, street sellers, chimney-sweepers, street-musicians, "mudlarks," "pure-finders," rag-gatherers, "running-patterers," dock laborers, cab-men, and hundreds of others, quoted directly in this massive work. An extraordinarily vital picture of London emerges. 110 illustrations. Total of lxxvi + 1951pp. 6⅝ x 10.

21934-8, 21935-6, 21936-4, 21937-2 Four volumes, Paperbound $16.00

HISTORY OF THE LATER ROMAN EMPIRE, J. B. Bury. Eloquent, detailed reconstruction of Western and Byzantine Roman Empire by a major historian, from the death of Theodosius I (395 A.D.) to the death of Justinian (565). Extensive quotations from contemporary sources; full coverage of important Roman and foreign figures of the time. xxxiv + 965pp. 20398-0, 20399-9 Two volumes, Paperbound $7.00

AN INTELLECTUAL AND CULTURAL HISTORY OF THE WESTERN WORLD, Harry Elmer Barnes. Monumental study, tracing the development of the accomplishments that make up human culture. Every aspect of man's achievement surveyed from its origins in the Paleolithic to the present day (1964); social structures, ideas, economic systems, art, literature, technology, mathematics, the sciences, medicine, religion, jurisprudence, etc. Evaluations of the contributions of scores of great men. 1964 edition, revised and edited by scholars in the many fields represented. Total of xxix + 1381pp. 21275-0, 21276-9, 21277-7 Three volumes, Paperbound $10.50

ADVENTURES OF AN AFRICAN SLAVER, Theodore Canot. Edited by Brantz Mayer. A detailed portrayal of slavery and the slave trade, 1820-1840. Canot, an established trader along the African coast, describes the slave economy of the African kingdoms, the treatment of captured negroes, the extensive journeys in the interior to gather slaves, slave revolts and their suppression, harems, bribes, and much more. Full and unabridged republication of 1854 edition. Introduction by Malcom Cowley. 16 illustrations. xvii + 448pp. 22456-2 Paperbound $3.50

MY BONDAGE AND MY FREEDOM, Frederick Douglass. Born and brought up in slavery, Douglass witnessed its horrors and experienced its cruelties, but went on to become one of the most outspoken forces in the American anti-slavery movement. Considered the best of his autobiographies, this book graphically describes the in-human treatment of slaves, its effects on slave owners and slave families, and how Douglass's determination led him to a new life. Unaltered reprint of 1st (1855) edition. xxxii + 464pp. 22457-0 Paperbound $2.50

THE INDIANS' BOOK, recorded and edited by Natalie Curtis. Lore, music, narratives, dozens of drawings by Indians themselves from an authoritative and important survey of native culture among Plains, Southwestern, Lake and Pueblo Indians. Standard work in popular ethnomusicology. 149 songs in full notation. 23 draw-ings, 23 photos. xxxi + 584pp. 6⅝ x 9⅜. 21939-9 Paperbound $4.50

DICTIONARY OF AMERICAN PORTRAITS, edited by Hayward and Blanche Cirker. 4024 portraits of 4000 most important Americans, colonial days to 1905 (with a few important categories, like Presidents, to present). Pioneers, explorers, colonial figures, U. S. officials, politicians, writers, military and naval men, scientists, inven-tors, manufacturers, jurists, actors, historians, educators, notorious figures, Indian chiefs, etc. All authentic contemporary likenesses. The only work of its kind in existence; supplements all biographical sources for libraries. Indispensable to any-one working with American history. 8,000-item classified index, finding lists, other aids. xiv + 756pp. 9¼ x 12¾. 21823-6 Clothbound $30.00

TRITTON'S GUIDE TO BETTER WINE AND BEER MAKING FOR BEGINNERS, S. M. Tritton. All you need to know to make family-sized quantities of over 100 types of grape, fruit, herb and vegetable wines; as well as beers, mead, cider, etc. Com-plete recipes, advice as to equipment, procedures such as fermenting, bottling, and storing wines. Recipes given in British, U. S., and metric measures. Accompanying booklet lists sources in U. S. A. where ingredients may be bought, and additional information. 11 illustrations. 157pp. 5⅝ x 8⅛.
(USO) 22090-7 Clothbound $3.50

GARDENING WITH HERBS FOR FLAVOR AND FRAGRANCE, Helen M. Fox. How to grow herbs in your own garden, how to use them in your cooking (over 55 recipes included), legends and myths associated with each species, uses in medicine, per-fumes, etc.—these are elements of one of the few books written especially for Amer-ican herb fanciers. Guides you step-by-step from soil preparation to harvesting and storage for each type of herb. 12 drawings by Louise Mansfield. xiv + 334pp.
22540-2 Paperbound $2.50

INCIDENTS OF TRAVEL IN YUCATAN, John L. Stephens. Classic (1843) exploration of jungles of Yucatan, looking for evidences of Maya civilization. Stephens found many ruins; comments on travel adventures, Mexican and Indian culture. 127 striking illustrations by F. Catherwood. Total of 669 pp.

20926-1, 20927-X Two volumes, Paperbound $5.00

INCIDENTS OF TRAVEL IN CENTRAL AMERICA, CHIAPAS, AND YUCATAN, John L. Stephens. An exciting travel journal and an important classic of archeology. Narrative relates his almost single-handed discovery of the Mayan culture, and exploration of the ruined cities of Copan, Palenque, Utatlan and others; the monuments they dug from the earth, the temples buried in the jungle, the customs of poverty-stricken Indians living a stone's throw from the ruined palaces. 115 drawings by F. Catherwood. Portrait of Stephens. xii + 812pp.

22404-X, 22405-8 Two volumes, Paperbound $6.00

A NEW VOYAGE ROUND THE WORLD, William Dampier. Late 17-century naturalist joined the pirates of the Spanish Main to gather information; remarkably vivid account of buccaneers, pirates; detailed, accurate account of botany, zoology, ethnography of lands visited. Probably the most important early English voyage, enormous implications for British exploration, trade, colonial policy. Also most interesting reading. Argonaut edition, introduction by Sir Albert Gray. New introduction by Percy Adams. 6 plates, 7 illustrations. xlvii + 376pp. 6½ x 9¼.

21900-3 Paperbound $3.00

INTERNATIONAL AIRLINE PHRASE BOOK IN SIX LANGUAGES, Joseph W. Bátor. Important phrases and sentences in English paralleled with French, German, Portuguese, Italian, Spanish equivalents, covering all possible airport-travel situations; created for airline personnel as well as tourist by Language Chief, Pan American Airlines. xiv + 204pp.

22017-6 Paperbound $2.00

STAGE COACH AND TAVERN DAYS, Alice Morse Earle. Detailed, lively account of the early days of taverns; their uses and importance in the social, political and military life; furnishings and decorations; locations; food and drink; tavern signs, etc. Second half covers every aspect of early travel; the roads, coaches, drivers, etc. Nostalgic, charming, packed with fascinating material. 157 illustrations, mostly photographs. xiv + 449pp.

22518-6 Paperbound $4.00

NORSE DISCOVERIES AND EXPLORATIONS IN NORTH AMERICA, Hjalmar R. Holand. The perplexing Kensington Stone, found in Minnesota at the end of the 19th century. Is it a record of a Scandinavian expedition to North America in the 14th century? Or is it one of the most successful hoaxes in history. A scientific detective investigation. Formerly *Westward from Vinland.* 31 photographs, 17 figures. x + 354pp.

22014-1 Paperbound $2.75

A BOOK OF OLD MAPS, compiled and edited by Emerson D. Fite and Archibald Freeman. 74 old maps offer an unusual survey of the discovery, settlement and growth of America down to the close of the Revolutionary war: maps showing Norse settlements in Greenland, the explorations of Columbus, Verrazano, Cabot, Champlain, Joliet, Drake, Hudson, etc., campaigns of Revolutionary war battles, and much more. Each map is accompanied by a brief historical essay. xvi + 299pp. 11 x 13¾.

22084-2 Paperbound $6.00

ALPHABETS AND ORNAMENTS, Ernst Lehner. Well-known pictorial source for decorative alphabets, script examples, cartouches, frames, decorative title pages, calligraphic initials, borders, similar material. 14th to 19th century, mostly European. Useful in almost any graphic arts designing, varied styles. 750 illustrations. 256pp. 7 x 10.   21905-4 Paperbound $4.00

PAINTING: A CREATIVE APPROACH, Norman Colquhoun. For the beginner simple guide provides an instructive approach to painting: major stumbling blocks for beginner; overcoming them, technical points; paints and pigments; oil painting; watercolor and other media and color. New section on "plastic" paints. Glossary. Formerly *Paint Your Own Pictures.* 221pp.   22000-1 Paperbound $1.75

THE ENJOYMENT AND USE OF COLOR, Walter Sargent. Explanation of the relations between colors themselves and between colors in nature and art, including hundreds of little-known facts about color values, intensities, effects of high and low illumination, complementary colors. Many practical hints for painters, references to great masters. 7 color plates, 29 illustrations. x + 274pp.

20944-X Paperbound $2.75

THE NOTEBOOKS OF LEONARDO DA VINCI, compiled and edited by Jean Paul Richter. 1566 extracts from original manuscripts reveal the full range of Leonardo's versatile genius: all his writings on painting, sculpture, architecture, anatomy, astronomy, geography, topography, physiology, mining, music, etc., in both Italian and English, with 186 plates of manuscript pages and more than 500 additional drawings. Includes studies for the Last Supper, the lost Sforza monument, and other works. Total of xlvii + 866pp. 7⅞ x 10¾.

22572-0, 22573-9 Two volumes, Paperbound $10.00

MONTGOMERY WARD CATALOGUE OF 1895. Tea gowns, yards of flannel and pillow-case lace, stereoscopes, books of gospel hymns, the New Improved Singer Sewing Machine, side saddles, milk skimmers, straight-edged razors, high-button shoes, spittoons, and on and on . . . listing some 25,000 items, practically all illustrated. Essential to the shoppers of the 1890's, it is our truest record of the spirit of the period. Unaltered reprint of Issue No. 57, Spring and Summer 1895. Introduction by Boris Emmet. Innumerable illustrations. xiii + 624pp. 8½ x 11⅝.

22377-9 Paperbound $6.95

THE CRYSTAL PALACE EXHIBITION ILLUSTRATED CATALOGUE (LONDON, 1851). One of the wonders of the modern world—the Crystal Palace Exhibition in which all the nations of the civilized world exhibited their achievements in the arts and sciences—presented in an equally important illustrated catalogue. More than 1700 items pictured with accompanying text—ceramics, textiles, cast-iron work, carpets, pianos, sleds, razors, wall-papers, billiard tables, beehives, silverware and hundreds of other artifacts—represent the focal point of Victorian culture in the Western World. Probably the largest collection of Victorian decorative art ever assembled— indispensable for antiquarians and designers. Unabridged republication of the Art-Journal Catalogue of the Great Exhibition of 1851, with all terminal essays. New introduction by John Gloag, F.S.A. xxxiv + 426pp. 9 x 12.

22503-8 Paperbound $4.50

THE ARCHITECTURE OF COUNTRY HOUSES, Andrew J. Downing. Together with Vaux's *Villas and Cottages* this is the basic book for Hudson River Gothic architecture of the middle Victorian period. Full, sound discussions of general aspects of housing, architecture, style, decoration, furnishing, together with scores of detailed house plans, illustrations of specific buildings, accompanied by full text. Perhaps the most influential single American architectural book. 1850 edition. Introduction by J. Stewart Johnson. 321 figures, 34 architectural designs. xvi + 560pp.
22003-6 Paperbound $4.00

LOST EXAMPLES OF COLONIAL ARCHITECTURE, John Mead Howells. Full-page photographs of buildings that have disappeared or been so altered as to be denatured, including many designed by major early American architects. 245 plates. xvii + 248pp. 7⅞ x 10¾. 21143-6 Paperbound $3.50

DOMESTIC ARCHITECTURE OF THE AMERICAN COLONIES AND OF THE EARLY REPUBLIC, Fiske Kimball. Foremost architect and restorer of Williamsburg and Monticello covers nearly 200 homes between 1620-1825. Architectural details, construction, style features, special fixtures, floor plans, etc. Generally considered finest work in its area. 219 illustrations of houses, doorways, windows, capital mantels. xx + 314pp. 7⅞ x 10¾. 21743-4 Paperbound $4.00

EARLY AMERICAN ROOMS: 1650-1858, edited by Russell Hawes Kettell. Tour of 12 rooms, each representative of a different era in American history and each furnished, decorated, designed and occupied in the style of the era. 72 plans and elevations, 8-page color section, etc., show fabrics, wall papers, arrangements, etc. Full descriptive text. xvii + 200pp. of text. 8⅜ x 11¼.
21633-0 Paperbound $5.00

THE FITZWILLIAM VIRGINAL BOOK, edited by J. Fuller Maitland and W. B. Squire. Full modern printing of famous early 17th-century ms. volume of 300 works by Morley, Byrd, Bull, Gibbons, etc. For piano or other modern keyboard instrument; easy to read format. xxxvi + 938pp. 8⅜ x 11.
21068-5, 21069-3 Two volumes, Paperbound $10.00

KEYBOARD MUSIC, Johann Sebastian Bach. Bach Gesellschaft edition. A rich selection of Bach's masterpieces for the harpsichord: the six English Suites, six French Suites, the six Partitas (Clavierübung part I), the Goldberg Variations (Clavierübung part IV), the fifteen Two-Part Inventions and the fifteen Three-Part Sinfonias. Clearly reproduced on large sheets with ample margins; eminently playable. vi + 312pp. 8⅛ x 11. 22360-4 Paperbound $5.00

THE MUSIC OF BACH: AN INTRODUCTION, Charles Sanford Terry. A fine, nontechnical introduction to Bach's music, both instrumental and vocal. Covers organ music, chamber music, passion music, other types. Analyzes themes, developments, innovations. x + 114pp. 21075-8 Paperbound $1.25

BEETHOVEN AND HIS NINE SYMPHONIES, Sir George Grove. Noted British musicologist provides best history, analysis, commentary on symphonies. Very thorough, rigorously accurate; necessary to both advanced student and amateur music lover. 436 musical passages. vii + 407 pp. 20334-4 Paperbound $2.75

FUNDAMENTAL FORMULAS OF PHYSICS, edited by Donald H. Menzel. Most useful reference and study work, ranges from simplest to most highly sophisticated operations. Individual chapters, with full texts explaining formulae, prepared by leading authorities cover basic mathematical formulas, statistics, nomograms, physical constants, classical mechanics, special theory of relativity, general theory of relativity, hydrodynamics and aerodynamics, boundary value problems in mathematical physics, heat and thermodynamics, statistical mechanics, kinetic theory of gases, viscosity, thermal conduction, electromagnetism, electronics, acoustics, geometrical optics, physical optics, electron optics, molecular spectra, atomic spectra, quantum mechanics, nuclear theory, cosmic rays and high energy phenomena, particle accelerators, solid state, magnetism, etc. Special chapters also cover physical chemistry, astrophysics, celestian mechanics, meteorology, and biophysics. Indispensable part of library of every scientist. Total of xli + 787pp.
60595-7, 60596-5 Two volumes, Paperbound $6.00

INTRODUCTION TO EXPERIMENTAL PHYSICS, William B. Fretter. Detailed coverage of techniques and equipment: measurements, vacuum tubes, pulse circuits, rectifiers, oscillators, magnet design, particle counters, nuclear emulsions, cloud chambers, accelerators, spectroscopy, magnetic resonance, x-ray diffraction, low temperature, etc. One of few books to cover laboratory hazards, design of exploratory experiments, measurements. 298 figures. xii + 349pp.
(EBE) 61890-0 Paperbound $3.00

CONCEPTS AND METHODS OF THEORETICAL PHYSICS, Robert Bruce Lindsay. Introduction to methods of theoretical physics, emphasizing development of physical concepts and analysis of methods. Part I proceeds from single particle to collections of particles to statistical method. Part II covers application of field concept to material and non-material media. Numerous exercises and examples. 76 illustrations. x + 515pp.
62354-8 Paperbound $4.00

AN ELEMENTARY TREATISE ON THEORETICAL MECHANICS, Sir James Jeans. Great scientific expositor in remarkably clear presentation of basic classical material: rest, motion, forces acting on particle, statics, motion of particle under variable force, motion of rigid bodies, coordinates, etc. Emphasizes explanation of fundamental physical principles rather than mathematics or applications. Hundreds of problems worked in text. 156 figures. x + 364pp. 61839-0 Paperbound $2.75

THEORETICAL MECHANICS: AN INTRODUCTION TO MATHEMATICAL PHYSICS, Joseph S. Ames and Francis D. Murnaghan. Mathematically rigorous introduction to vector and tensor methods, dynamics, harmonic vibrations, gyroscopic theory, principle of least constraint, Lorentz-Einstein transformation. 159 problems; many fully-worked examples. 39 figures. ix + 462pp. 60461-6 Paperbound $3.50

THE PRINCIPLE OF RELATIVITY, Albert Einstein, Hendrick A. Lorentz, Hermann Minkowski and Hermann Weyl. Eleven original papers on the special and general theory of relativity, all unabridged. Seven papers by Einstein, two by Lorentz, one each by Minkowski and Weyl. "A thrill to read again the original papers by these giants," *School Science and Mathematics.* Translated by W. Perret and G. B. Jeffery. Notes by A. Sommerfeld. 7 diagrams. viii + 216pp.
60081-5 Paperbound $2.25

MATHEMATICAL PUZZLES FOR BEGINNERS AND ENTHUSIASTS, Geoffrey Mott-Smith. 189 puzzles from easy to difficult—involving arithmetic, logic, algebra, properties of digits, probability, etc.—for enjoyment and mental stimulus. Explanation of mathematical principles behind the puzzles. 135 illustrations. viii + 248pp.

20198-8 Paperbound $1.75

PAPER FOLDING FOR BEGINNERS, William D. Murray and Francis J. Rigney. Easiest book on the market, clearest instructions on making interesting, beautiful origami. Sail boats, cups, roosters, frogs that move legs, bonbon boxes, standing birds, etc. 40 projects; more than 275 diagrams and photographs. 94pp.

20713-7 Paperbound $1.00

TRICKS AND GAMES ON THE POOL TABLE, Fred Herrmann. 79 tricks and games— some solitaires, some for two or more players, some competitive games—to entertain you between formal games. Mystifying shots and throws, unusual caroms, tricks involving such props as cork, coins, a hat, etc. Formerly *Fun on the Pool Table*. 77 figures. 95pp.

21814-7 Paperbound $1.00

HAND SHADOWS TO BE THROWN UPON THE WALL: A SERIES OF NOVEL AND AMUSING FIGURES FORMED BY THE HAND, Henry Bursill. Delightful picturebook from great-grandfather's day shows how to make 18 different hand shadows: a bird that flies, duck that quacks, dog that wags his tail, camel, goose, deer, boy, turtle, etc. Only book of its sort. vi + 33pp. 6½ x 9¼. 21779-5 Paperbound $1.00

WHITTLING AND WOODCARVING, E. J. Tangerman. 18th printing of best book on market. "If you can cut a potato you can carve" toys and puzzles, chains, chessmen, caricatures, masks, frames, woodcut blocks, surface patterns, much more. Information on tools, woods, techniques. Also goes into serious wood sculpture from Middle Ages to present, East and West. 464 photos, figures. x + 293pp.

20965-2 Paperbound $2.00

HISTORY OF PHILOSOPHY, Julián Marias. Possibly the clearest, most easily followed, best planned, most useful one-volume history of philosophy on the market; neither skimpy nor overfull. Full details on system of every major philosopher and dozens of less important thinkers from pre-Socratics up to Existentialism and later. Strong on many European figures usually omitted. Has gone through dozens of editions in Europe. 1966 edition, translated by Stanley Appelbaum and Clarence Strowbridge. xviii + 505pp.

21739-6 Paperbound $3.00

YOGA: A SCIENTIFIC EVALUATION, Kovoor T. Behanan. Scientific but non-technical study of physiological results of yoga exercises; done under auspices of Yale U. Relations to Indian thought, to psychoanalysis, etc. 16 photos. xxiii + 270pp.

20505-3 Paperbound $2.50

Prices subject to change without notice.
Available at your book dealer or write for free catalogue to Dept. GI, Dover Publications, Inc., 180 Varick St., N. Y., N. Y. 10014. Dover publishes more than 150 books each year on science, elementary and advanced mathematics, biology, music, art, literary history, social sciences and other areas.